Messiah REVEALED
in PURIM

by

Hannah Nesher

Scripture quotations are taken from the Hebrew-English Bible. Copyright © by Bible Society in Israel 1996 and the Israel Association for the Dissemination of Biblical Writings. The Bible Society in Israel, P.O. Box 44 Jerusalem, 91000 Israel

Scripture quotations taken from the HOLY BIBLE, NEW INTERNATIONAL VERSION. Copyright © 1973, 1978, 1984 by International Bible Society. Used by permission of Zondervan Publishing House.

ISBN# 978-0-9733892-7-2

For speaking engagements please contact Hannah:

> Hannah Nesher, Voice for Israel
> Suite #313- 11215 Jasper Ave.
> Edmonton, Alberta
> T5K 0L5 Canada

> www.voiceforisrael.net

Copyright © 2008 by Voice for Israel

All rights reserved under International Copyright Law. Contents and/or cover may not be reproduced in whole or in part in any form without the express written consent of the Publisher.

Cover design by James Vanderwekken - jvnderwe@hotmail.com

DEDICATION

To the God of my fathers, Avraham, Yitzchak and Yaacov,

יהוה
אהיה אשר אהיה

To You whose name says

You will be whoever You will be –

Thanks for being all I have ever needed!

And to Your Son and Messiah Y'shuah

ישוע

For your obedience to the Father

For being led like a lamb to the slaughter

For pouring out your soul unto death

So that I could live!

A Special Thank You

I would like to say *todah rabah* (thanks very much) and publicly acknowledge my debt of gratitude towards some of the many people who helped with this work.

First of all, to my mother and father who gave me life. Thank you for your courage in training up this daughter of yours through all our ups and downs. Although we may not always agree on theology, your love has remained constant.

To David, for applying your excellent technical skills to help bring this book to publication. Thank you for your love, encouragment and steadfast faith - and for the gift of our two wonderful children.

To my children, Clayton, Courtney, Timothy, Liat, and Avi-ad, who each supplied material and inspiration for my writing. Thanks for your patience with the crazy times in our family - for loving and forgiving me. Big hugs to Clayton for his great technical support.

To our ministry partners for your faithful love, fervent prayers and generous support. May you be fully rewarded by the God of Israel under whose wings you have taken refuge - Ruth 2:12

To James Vanderwekken for his awesome graphic design work and technical support. You are a treasure!

To Denis Vanderwekken & his late wife, Corrie for their friendship, support, and help in the journey. Corrie - I miss you!
To Marilyn for your intercession & willingness to proofread.

Most of all, to the Holy Spirit (Ruach Hakodesh), for giving me the inspiration, motivation, and words to write.

Todah rabah! (thanks so much!) תודה רבה

Contents

Words You Need to Know..8

1. **Purim - Biblical Family Fun**..................................9
   - The History of Purim.......................................10
   - Trick or Treat?..14
   - Why Celebrate Purim?....................................18
   - Gentiles for Yeshua...19
   - God's Appointed Times...................................23
   - Festivals of Our Own Choosing......................24
   - War with the Amalekites.................................26

2. **Esther, Amalek, and Terrorism**............................28
   - Arafat and the PLO...30
   - Foundation of Deception................................32
   - God Issues a Warning....................................34
   - Facts & Myths About Israel & the Palestinians...35
   - Suicide Warriors Pretty in Pink.......................36
   - Islam and World Unity....................................38

3. **A Jew is Taking Over the World**...........................41
   - Christians Also Misled...................................43
   - Anti-Semitism North-American Style.............44
   - Esther and Exile...46
   - Responsibility of the Church..........................47
   - He Who Keepeth Israel
   - Neither Slumbers nor Sleeps.........................49
   - Judgement on the gods of Egypt...................51
   - The Second Exodus......................................53

4	**The Arm of the Lord**..................................**55**	
	Isaiah 53 - King Messiah..................................56	
	What Will God Do?..58	
	I Will Bless Those Who Bless You....................59	
	Be Careful How You	
	Touch the Apple of God's Eye..........................60	
	Curse vs. Curse..61	
	Cursing in the Church......................................62	
	The Rise of Anti-Semitism in the Church........63	
5	**Replacement Theology**..............................**65**	
	Quotes of the Church Fathers..........................68	
	Jews - Christ Killers?.......................................69	
	Why Can't Jews 'See' Jesus?............................73	
	The Attitude of Martin Luther Towards the Jews...........77	
	'Judensau'..78	
	Missionary Go Home!......................................80	
	The Christian Evangelism Under Attack.........80	
	Hitler Borrows Doctrine from the Church......82	
	Love One Another..83	
6	**Response of the Nations**............................**85**	
	Prelude to Holocaust - Evian..........................85	
	Kristallnacht..92	
	German Reaction to Evian..............................93	
7	**Remember Amalek!**..................................**98**	
	Curses of the Mosaic Covenant......................99	
	A Day of Vengeance - To Uphold Zion's Cause...........102	

	Judgement of the Nations...106	
	Justice and Mercy...108	
	The Abrahamic Covenant..110	
	Not For Your Sake...111	
8	**The Set Time For Mercy on Zion**..............................113	
	End of the Punishment..113	
	Seven Times..114	
	Times of the Gentiles Fulfilled......................................115	
	The Budding of the Fig Tree...117	
	Say to Zion...Your God is Here!...................................121	
9	**God - The Covenant Keeper**...124	
	The Scarlet Cord - Salvation for Rahab........................125	
	Separating Sheep and Goats..126	
	Chuck & Ted...127	
10	**Personal Salvation the New Covenant**.....................129	
11	**Mordechai's Call to Esther**..132	
	Sorrow Turned to Joy..137	

Appendix I..138
Appendix II...144
Appendix III..146
Appendix IV..150

Words You Need to Know

Purim – Festival of Lots, named for the number used by Haman to choose a day to kill the Jews.

Megillah – scroll of the story of Queen Esther.

Grogger – noisemaker – the Hebrew word is "ra-ashan".

Hamantaschen – cookie filled with dried prunes, raisins, or poppyseeds; in Hebrew the cookies are called Oznei Haman, which means Haman's ears.

Shalach Manot – exchange of cookies, fruit, and other treats among friends and neighbors. The words mean "sending gifts", from the command to send presents to one another and give gifts to the poor. (Esth. 9:22)

Queen Esther – the Jewish heroine.

Mordechai – Esther's cousin who raised her.

Haman – the wicked prime minister of Persia King Ahashverosh – ruler of Persia.

CHAPTER ONE

PURIM – BIBLICAL FAMILY FUN

Purim is a peculiar Biblical festival, often neglected and overlooked by the Christian church; it contains abundant truths for all people devoted to the God of Israel - Jew or Gentile. Unlike the other Feasts of the Lord, this celebration is not commanded in the book of Leviticus, chapter 23. Rather, it was a custom mandated by Mordechai, and established by the Jews of the time, that they and their descendants would never fail to celebrate the festival of Purim according to written instructions and at the prescribed time. (Esther 9:27)

For over two thousand years, Jewish people have celebrated Purim on the 14th (and sometimes 15th) day of the Hebrew month of Adar (February/March). This is the time in the yearly cycle of festivals where many Jewish people gather together in synagogues and homes to rejoice – to celebrate God's deliverance of His people in Persia from the forces of anti-Semitism, as recorded in the book of Esther.

It is a festival that especially invites children and adults alike to have fun and even indulge in a little silliness. The leader reads the entire book of Esther out loud in Hebrew, (called the reading of the Megilla), while the congregation participates by loudly 'booing', stomping their feet, and making a terrible noise with their 'groggers' (noisemakers or raashanim) whenever the name of the villain, Haman (Boooooo!!!!!!!) is mentioned. This custom originates in the Lord's word to Moses,

> **"I will completely blot out the memory of Amalek from under heaven"** (Ex. 17:14),

and

> **"The Lord will be at war against the Amalekites from generation to generation."** (v. 16)

Since Haman, the villain of the book of Esther, descended from the detestable Amalekites, who attacked the fledgling nation of Israel as Moses led them out of Egypt, the Jewish people join in pronouncing God's judgment upon the very name of Haman. This is a particularly Jewish form of spiritual warfare!

The History of Purim

The story of Purim takes place in the land of Persia (modern day Iran), after the decree had been declared allowing Judah to return from exile to Israel. The account of the return of the Jews from their Babylonian captivity is recorded in the book of Ezra (1-6). Many Jewish families, however, were well established and therefore chose to remain in Persia, among them Mordechai and Esther. Ahashverosh, king of Persia, ruled over 127 provinces, stretching from India to Ethiopia. Fond of wine, women, and song, Ahashverosh arranged elaborate banquet. When his queen, Vashti, refused to come and show off her beauty before the assembly, he had her banished from the kingdom and sought a new queen. This stands as a strong warning to women to obey the word of God in submitting to their husbands.

After what was probably the grandest beauty pageant of all times, the king chose a beautiful Jewish woman, whose Hebrew name was Hadassah (meaning myrtle), and in Persian was called Esther (Star). Upon the advice of her cousin, Mordechai, who raised her after the death of her parents, she concealed her Jewish identity until the appointed time. And so the Jews who remained in Persia felt secure, comfortable, and prosperous – they even had a Jewish queen on the throne. But just then, the enemy arose to carry out his evil plans. This time it was in the form of Haman, a descendant of the Jew-hating tribe of Amalek.

Haman, the prideful, vain Prime Minister to the king, demanded that everyone in the kingdom bow unto him. But only Mordechai, who was a devout Jew, refused to bow or worship anyone but his God. In retaliation, Haman, (true to his heritage), devised a scheme to solve 'the Jewish problem' once and for all, by annihilating every Jew - men, women, and children - throughout the empire, in a single day.

The festival derives its name because "lots" - *pur-im* – were cast to determine the exact date on which the Persians would destroy the Jews. Haman duped the king into allowing this genocide by perpetuating a lie that the Jews were vile creatures, disloyal to the king's authority.

An interesting note about the book of Esther is that God is not once directly mentioned in the text. And yet his actions show us that He is at work 'behind the scenes'. We see His divine intervention when Esther's cousin, Mordechai, "just happens" to discover a plot to overthrow the king and passes this bad news on to Esther. She in turn tells the king who records Mordechai's saving of the king's life in his book and has the rebels hanged.

Haman's plot to destroy the Jews of Persia almost worked – except for God working through the brave actions of Mordechai and Esther. Upon hearing of the king's edict to allow the destruction of his people, Mordechai donned sackcloth and ashes. He then appealed to Esther, the queen, to approach the king and beg his mercy. This unprecedented act of coming into the presence of the king without an explicit invitation could have cost Esther her life, for unless the king held out his golden scepter, Esther would have been executed. Mordechai warned his dear cousin Hadassah that her life as a Jewess would also be in danger; that she would probably not be spared simply by her dwelling in the royal palace. He exhorted her that if she kept silent, salvation would surely come for the Jews from another source, but that surely she had been raised to royal position by God Himself, exactly for such a time as this. By fulfilling her divine destiny, Esther would play a major role in helping to save her people from complete destruction. Although Esther feared the king, she obeyed Mordechai, as she had all her life.

Being a wise woman, Esther did not bring her request before the king immediately. She first undertook a three-day fast and called all the Jews of the kingdom to join her. Next, she dressed in her royal clothes and stood in the inner court of the King's house. The King extended his royal scepter to the queen, thereby granting her permission to approach him. Esther made her request known, and invited the king and Haman to a banquet. Which woman of any discernment does not know that the way to a man's heart is often through his stomach? Another interesting point to ponder is that Esther did not reveal her secret at the first banquet, but invited the men to a second banquet the next day. Did this allow Esther a night with the king to further soften his heart? There is another way besides's food to a man's heart! ☺

God was also at work, giving the king a terrible case of insomnia that night. In order to pass the time, the king called for his royal record books and in it, noticed that Mordechai had, in the past, saved his life. Immediately, he called in Haman. *"What should be done for the man the king chooses to honor?"*, he asked Haman. And Haman, being the conceited, egocentric man he was, assumed the king was speaking of him, therefore he suggested, *"Let him be seated on the king's own horse, the royal crown on his head, and let the first man of the kingdom stride before him, leading his horse."* You can imagine his humiliation when Haman later found himself leading his arch enemy, the Jew Mordechai, on the king's royal horse! This only further fueled his hatred against the Jews, but once again, female wisdom tried to save the day. Haman's wife, knowing that Haman had already built a set of gallows upon which he planned to hang Mordechai advised her husband that since he is fighting against someone of Jewish descent, he is fighting against God and will surely be ruined.

At the second banquet, Esther revealed the satanic plot against the Jews and her own affiliation with the Jewish people. She pleaded for her own life and for the salvation of her people. Although the king could not revoke his own decree, according to the laws of the Medes and Persians, he issued a second one, giving the Jews the right to arm and defend themselves. On the same day that Haman had planned to destroy all the Jews of Persia, God gave His people the victory.

> **"Thus the Jews defeated all their enemies with the stroke of the sword, with slaughter and destruction, and did what they pleased with those who hated them."** (Esth. 9:5)

Haman was hanged on the very gallows that he had prepared for Mordechai and his sons were all hanged. God reversed the curse; it came upon his own head.

To all of us who are in covenant with the God of Israel, and to those who bless the people of Israel, this story of Purim is good news. But to all those who oppose or hate the Jewish people, the story of Purim stands as a stark warning. Purim affirms the Biblical law that God blesses those who bless His people, and curses those who curse them. (Gen. 12:3) Thus the Purim story is directly relevant to our contemporary world, and especially with regards to the situation existing today in the Middle East. One does not have to look far to find Haman's modern-day heirs. They perhaps call themselves by different names, but their evil intent is the same – to erase the Jewish people and the nation of Israel from the face of the earth. Each time the enemies of Israel rise up against us, their schemes are foiled by the miraculous, 'behind the scenes' actions of our God. The Persian Gulf War ended victoriously on Purim, 5751.

Trick or Treat?

At Purim time, groups often perform a drama, re-enacting the events of the Book of Esther, and present it to the congregation. We once performed a 'modern-day version of the play for a Pentecostal church. The best part of the play, in my opinion as director, was when 'Haman' fell upon Esther, reclining on a makeshift lawn chair, knocking the whole thing over, and pleading for his life. He ad-libbed, *"Have mercy on me, I come from a dysfunctional family!"* It was not in the script, but the audience roared with laughter. I think we need to tear down the lie that God does not want His people to have fun and enjoy themselves. As an added twist, the woman who played the part of Esther eventually married the man who played the part of Haman. Esther marrying Haman?! God really does have a sense of humor. ☺ Dressing up in costume is part of the fun. Little girls wear crowns, tiaras and beautiful gowns, imagining themselves to be the lovely Queen Esther. The boys can either dress as the king, the righteous Mordechai, or even the bad guy – the evil Haman.

Today, we also have many well-meaning people, allowing their children to dress up in a costume and participate in the non-Biblical festival of Halloween, even though its origin is pagan, and its symbols glorify the forces of darkness against which we as believers, should be taking a stand.

Many churches, I have been grieved to discover, participate in this pagan festival of Halloween to a greater or lesser extent. At a church where we were teaching a series on 'Exploring the Jewish Roots of the Christian Faith', an alternative class down the hall was teaching how to carve pumpkins. The evil looking faces carved into the pumpkin represent demonic entities, damned souls, or the god of Saman. Candle lit pumpkins (jack o' lanterns) or skulls in a home originally meant that the residents were sympathetic to Satan and would therefore receive mercy from spirits and trick or treaters on their Halloween rounds. The pumpkin was left on people's doorsteps to demand the sacrifice of a virgin. If none was forthcoming (the treat), then the occupants of the household would receive a curse (the trick). They would leave a hexagram drawn in blood on the front door to attract demons.

Although the Druid religion was outlawed around 98-180 A.D. it moved underground and is still alive and active today, as evidenced by the widespread celebration of its holiest day of the year. Surveys show that educational systems, schools, and colleges put more money, time and effort into Halloween than any other school celebration. Before registering my son in the local kindergarten, I decided to speak with the teacher about this issue. I told her that it is against our beliefs and values to have my son participating in a festival against God, and I asked that he be excused. *"Well,"* she answered, *"I just don't see how this would be possible, since the entire month of October is spent in some kind of preparation for Halloween. Every day, the children either color a picture or make some kind of craft about witches, or else I read them a related storybook about Halloween."*

When I reminded her that God hates this sort of thing, she assured me that it's all right because "the children don't know what they're doing." (I thanked her very much for sharing and decided to home school my son!)

I suppose it is understandable that a heathen, unbelieving world would join with witches, druids, sorcerers and all other satanic worshippers in celebrating Halloween, but people of God? Members of my family consider themselves religious Orthodox Jews. In fact, some would say that they are fanatical in their observance of Rabbinical Judaism. When October 31st rolls around however, their children are out there in costume with the rest of the heathens gathering their sack of candies. One year, one of the older children happened to be present when I refused to allow my son to accept a Halloween pencil from my parents. Although I had determined 'not to preach' at them, my mother seemed to sincerely want to understand why I wouldn't take such an 'innocent thing' as a pencil. When my niece heard the explanation of the origin of these symbols of darkness and of Halloween itself, and God's word against it, she went pale and asked to go straight home. I know of tracts, books, and information warning people about Halloween, but to my dismay, these are all directed towards the Christian, as if the Bible does not first warn the Jews against such occult practices. This is also a subtler form of anti-Semitism – to say that the Bible tells 'Christians' not to participate in occultism completely excludes the Jews from inclusion as the people of God. I'm not letting Jews off the hook. As chosen, holy people of God, they should also know better, but unfortunately, many Jewish people have never read through the Old Testament Bible. Born again, Bible believing, church-going Christians who allow their children to dress up and participate in Halloween, however, are another story (even if they are celebrating in a church!).

In another church, we were teaching a series on the Feasts of the Lord as well as Messianic Jewish Dance. One week during the fall, we found that we were unable to teach in the usual hall since this had been converted into a makeshift 'haunted house'. A Canadian Christian Bible College where I was teaching an introductory Hebrew course advertised a Halloween 'Pumpkin Fun Race' for its students – future ministers for the Lord! Although most people consider this simply 'harmless fun', the Bible asks:

> **"What fellowship can light have with darkness?...**
> **Therefore come out from them and be separate,**
> **touch no unclean thing, and I will receive you,**
> **I will be a Father to you, and you will be my**
> **sons and daughters, says the Lord Almighty."**
> (2 Cor. 6:14-18)

In order to qualify as sons and daughters of the living God, we must pay a price. This is our separation from the darkness and paganism of the world – the commitment to live as holy people. This is a grave concern for the people of God. I have wondered, what would happen at this time of the year, if the angel of death flew over our towns and cities. At the first Passover, in ancient Egypt, when 'the destroyer' saw the blood, it passed over those homes and did not enter within. What if the angel of death was to fly over our homes during the month of October? Would he see the blood of the Lamb, or would He see symbols of darkness – windows and doors decorated with witches, ghouls, and other demonic figures? In this last hour, we can no longer keep a foot in each kingdom; we must make it clear where we stand. We must stand in the Kingdom of Light, not darkness!

> "The sacrifices of pagans are offered to demons, not to God, and I do not want you to be participants with demons. You cannot drink the cup of the Lord and the cup of demons too; you cannot have a part in both the Lord's table and the table of demons. Are we trying to arouse the Lord's jealousy? Are we stronger than He?" (1 Cor. 10:20-22)

What are we really trying to do in compromising our biblical faith with pagan festivals and rituals? One way of being clear about which side we are on is to forsake all elements of paganism (such as celebrating Halloween), and instead celebrate the Biblical Feasts (like Purim). Who needs 'Power Rangers' and 'Ninja Turtles'? Purim provides an opportunity for children (and adults) to dress up in costume and celebrate in a God-pleasing manner. One of the very sad things that we have come to discover about Israel is that, in attempting to be 'like the Gentile nations', it has merged its celebration of Purim with Halloween. Long before the actual festival, stores begin to fill their shelves with demonic costumes, imported from Western countries. Jewish children are just as likely to dress up as demons, ghosts, witches and vampires, as Mordechai, Esther, or the King. Truly such things should never be!

Why Celebrate Purim?

The Book of Esther in the Bible states,

> "These days should be remembered and observed in every generation by every family, and in every province and in every city. And these days of Purim should never cease to be celebrated by the Jews, nor should the memory of them die out among their descendants." (Esth. 9:28)

'Oh, well that is just for the Jews, not for us Christians', you may say. Is it? The Bible says:

> "The Jews took it upon themselves to establish the custom that they and their descendants and <u>all who join them</u> should without fail observe these two days every year, in the way prescribed and at the time appointed." (Esth. 9:27)

Who are Christians if not those who have joined the Jewish people through Yeshua Hamashiach, (translated as Jesus the Messiah, or the 'Christ'). To be a Christian is to be a follower of Christ; Christ is not a name, but a title that comes from the Greek language, meaning 'anointed one' or Messiah (in Hebrew. Mashiah משיח) Therefore, a Christian is a follower of the Jewish Messiah, whose real name is Yeshua. I believe that this has profound significance for the body of the Messiah, and that the Church is beginning to wake up to this revelation from the Holy Spirit.

Gentiles For Yeshua

The book of Romans explain the relationship of gentile Christians to their Jewish brothers and sisters through the analogy of an olive tree:

> "...You, though a wild olive shoot, have been grafted in among the others and now share in the nourishing sap from the olive root, do not boast... You do not support the root, but the root supports you." (Rom. 11:17-18)

There are not two separate roots – one for Christians and one for Jews. Both are firmly rooted into the God of Israel through divine covenant. Christians are to remember their Jewish roots, their connection to the God of Israel and His covenant people, the nation of Israel. When I teach about 'Jewish Roots', I sometimes hear people spit out the venomous words, *"Oh, those Jews think they're so special!"* But it is God who has said they are His treasured possession. This is not my opinion, this is what the Bible says.

> **"For you are a holy people to the Lord your God; the Lord your God has chosen you to be a people for Himself, a special treasure above all the peoples on the face of the earth. The Lord did not set His love on you nor choose you because you were more in number than any other people, for you were the least of all peoples; but because the Lord loves you, and because He would keep the oath which He swore to your fathers..."** (Deut. 7:6-8)

Praise God that now anyone of any race, tongue, or tribe may qualify as one of God's 'holy, chosen treasure' along with the Jewish people.

> **"But you are a chosen people, a royal priesthood, a holy nation, a people belonging to God, that you may declare the praises of him who called you out of darkness into his wonderful light. Once you were not a people, but now you are the people of God; once you had not received mercy, but now you have received mercy."** (1 Pet. 2:9-10)

This is the wonderful creative act of God – creating one people out of two – "People of the God of Abraham."

> "The nobles of the nations assemble as the people of the God of Abraham." (Ps. 47:9)

The dividing wall (the machitzah) has been broken down, through the blood of our Messiah:

> "For he himself is our peace, who has made the two one and has destroyed the barrier, the dividing wall of hostility, by abolishing in his flesh the (sacrificial) law with its commandments and regulations. His purpose was to create in himself one new man out of the two, thus making peace, and in this one body to reconcile both of them to God through the cross, by which he put to death their hostility." (Eph. 2:14-16)

A wall of partition was used to prevent Gentiles, who were at that time considered unclean, from entering the inner court of the Temple. But one glorious, historic Shavuot (Pentecost), God gave Peter a vision and showed him that we are not to call any *man* unclean whom God has made clean through the blood of His son (Acts 10:28).

> "God does not show favoritism, but accepts men from every nation who fear him and do what is right." (Acts 10:34)

The true meaning of this vision deals with people and spiritual purification, not food, as many Christians believe. This chapter of Acts does not stand as a blanket annulment of God's word regarding clean and unclean foods. God did not all of a sudden change his mind or reconsider the wisdom of His words. Our digestive systems did not suddenly become transformed at the cross. God first chose the nation of Israel; He entrusted them first with the Torah, His word, and also sent the Messiah to them first. Yeshua said,

> "**I was sent only to the lost sheep of the house of Israel.**" (Matt. 15:24)

Yes, the New Covenant was first established with the house of Israel and the house of Judah (Jer. 31:31).

Paul says,

> "**I am not ashamed of the gospel, because it is the power of God for the salvation of everyone who believes; first for the Jew, then for the Gentile.**" (Rom. 1:16)

This is a matter of chronology, not preference. The ancient, Hebrew prophet knew, through revelation of the Holy Spirit, that the Messiah would not contain His salvation for Israel alone.

> "**It is too small a thing for you to be my servant to restore the tribes of Jacob and bring back those of Israel I have kept. I will also make you a light for the Gentiles, that you may bring my salvation to the ends of the earth.**" (Is. 49:6)

What I am attempting to do is use the sword of the Spirit, which is the word of God, to cut through some well-established lies, and lay the foundation of truth about the Christian's relationship to Israel and the Jewish people. Gentiles used to be "**...separate from the Messiah, excluded from citizenship in Israel, foreigners to the covenants of the promise, without hope and without God in the world.**" (Eph. 2:12)

But now in the Messiah Yeshua, those who were once far away have been brought near to God through the blood of the Messiah – through covenant – adopted into the family of God and joined forever to Israel and the Jewish people.

> **"Consequently, you are no longer foreigners and aliens, but fellow citizens with God's people and members of God's household"** (Eph. 2:19)

God's Appointed Times

If the Messiah broke down the dividing wall between Jew and Gentile, why does the machitzah still seems to be in place? Could a partial, if not significant, answer be that Christians have created their own sets of rules and regulations, apart from the Word of God? By celebrating 'Christian' festivals, as distinct from the Biblical Feasts, have they once again purposefully separated themselves from their Jewish brothers and sisters and re-built that dividing wall which Yeshua purposed to be destroyed?

There seems to be such an emphasis on grace in some churches today, that people are forgetting our God is a God of peace and order, not chaos, and everyone is not free to do whatever 'feels right'. God has His appointed times and ways. He is like a master craftsman, who has set specific precious gems and jewels on the dial face of an exquisite divine timepiece. For us to change the nature of His jewels or to move them into our own design cannot add, but only detract from God's wisdom. The prophetic book of Daniel tells us that the coming anti-Christ, as part of his evil program to wage war against the Most High God and His saints, will

> **"...try to change the set times and the laws."**
> (Dan. 7:25)

Therefore, I ask you a question (in true Jewish fashion): *"In what spirit are the people who have succeeded in changing God's appointed times – His feasts and festivals – into their own man-made versions at times of their own choosing?"*

Festivals of Our Own Choosing

The Bible gives us an example of a King who instituted his own 'Festival to the Lord', and God's displeasure with his actions. King Jeroboam:

> **"Instituted a festival on the fifteenth day of the eighth month, like the festival held in Judah…On the fifteenth day of the eight month, a month of his own choosing, he offered sacrifices on the altar he had built at Bethel. So he instituted the festival for the Israelites and went up to the altar to make offerings."** (1 Kings 12:32-33)

We know that today, most Christians celebrate festivals such as Christmas and Easter that are not mentioned in the Bible. From where do these festivals originate? They were the month and day of a man's own choosing. The Roman Emperor Constantine, in the fourth century, accommodated the already existing pagan dates of worshipping false gods. Some people take the view that this no longer matters; that we should not fault people for celebrating these dates since their intention is to honor the Lord. Since when, however, has sincerity been an excuse for falsehood? Many 'New Agers' are completely sincere in their beliefs as well, believing (as I once did) that this is the pathway to God. This does not prevent their practices from being an abomination to the Lord!

When Aaron built a golden calf for the Israelites at Mt. Sinai, he did not say, 'let's celebrate a pagan festival to a foreign god'; instead he announced,

> **"Tomorrow there will be a festival to the Lord"**
> (Ex. 32:5)

And after sacrificing burnt offerings, they sat down to eat and drink and got up to indulge in revelry. The Lord sent Moses down the mountain because the people had become corrupt. He was so angry that the Lord's desire was only to be left alone so that He could destroy the whole nation and start over again with Moses. But Moses interceded for the people and the Lord relented from bringing the disaster he had threatened upon the people (Ex. 32:6-14). Today, the corruption of paganism remains in the Christian Church and the Lord wants to cleanse and purify His bride. We need, also, to recognize this sin and to intercede on her behalf.

> **"Remove falsehood and lies far from me"**
> (Prov. 30:8)

May this be our hearts' cry in this hour as well. I remember one woman attending a class in which I was teaching this information. I noticed her weeping in the back of the room. Later, I spoke with her and she told me that at first, she said to herself, *"Surely what we are doing as an entire body of Christians could not be that bad."* And so she asked the Lord to show her if these things really are detestable to Him or not. In response, what the Lord showed her brought her into the deep sorrow of true repentance. But repentance does not simply mean emotion; it means actual change.

War With the Amalekites

Purim gives another example of the consequences of 'doing our own thing'. God commanded King Saul to completely destroy the Amalekites for what they did to Israel.

> **"This is what the Lord Almighty says: 'I will punish the Amalekites for what they did to Israel when they waylaid them as they came up from Egypt. Now go, attack the Amalekites and totally destroy everything that belongs to them. Do not spare them; put to death men and women, children and infants, cattle and sheep, camels and donkeys."** (1 Sam. 15:2-3)

What could the Amalekites possibly have done to Israel to warrant such severe judgment from the Lord? For this, we need to look back into the book of Exodus.

> **"The Amalekites came and attacked the Israelites at Rephidim."** (Ex. 17:8)

What was God's response to this unwarranted attack on his fledgling nation of Israel, wandering in the desert wilderness after escaping the bondage of Egypt?

God said,

> **"I will completely blot out the memory of Amalek from under heaven."** (Ex. 17:14)

This is the place where an altar was built called, 'יהוה NISSI', (Adonai is my Banner. The root word, 'Nes', is also the Hebrew word for 'miracle'). It was declared here that:

> **"The Lord will be at war against the Amalekites from generation to generation."** (Ex. 17:15)

What is the connection between Amalek and Purim? Haman, the anti-Semitic villain in the book of Esther, is a direct descendant of King Agag of the Amalekites. King Saul spared this King's life, contrary to the clear command of the Lord to destroy Amalek completely. Because of Saul's half-hearted obedience to God, this one Amalekite survived to produce offspring that would threaten the Jewish people once again. We can see from this that our obedience or disobedience to the commandments of God may have significant consequences reaching far beyond what we could ever imagine. The Spirit of Amalek is still alive and well today. The Lord is still at war with the Amalekites.

CHAPTER TWO

ESTHER, AMALEK, AND TERRORISM

> **"How can I endure to see the evil that shall come unto my people? Or how can I endure to see the destruction of my kindred?"** (Esth. 8:6)

On the night of March 4th, 1996, Jewish people in homes and synagogues around the world read these words as part of the reading of the Megillah (the book of Esther). This corresponds to the date 2,500 years prior, the 13th of the Biblical month of Adar, which Haman selected by lots (Purim) as the date he would kill all the Jews in the Babylonian Empire. Every year since this time, the Biblical Feast of Purim is celebrated with great rejoicing to commemorate God's deliverance of His people from the forces of anti-Semitism.

> "But not this year (1999). Just before sunrise, a day before the beginning of the celebrations, a terrorist boarded a bus on route 18 in Jerusalem and detonated a bomb he was wearing, killing passengers and himself. In Tel Aviv the next day, another suicide bomber blew himself up outside the popular Dizengoff Shopping Center.

> The nation of Israel was thrown into shock again, barely recovered from similar bombings on February 25. In all, 62 adults and children were killed, and hundreds were injured. Security sources reveal that there are hundreds more teenagers and young men eager to offer their lives for Allah, and to kill Jews, in order to enter the Muslim paradise and be welcomed by 72 virgins to satisfy their desires."[1]

Was it just a coincidence that for two years in a row, these terrorist bombings came at the exact time that Haman attempted to exterminate the Jewish people 2,500 years earlier? I don't think so. The same spirit that was in Amalek that caused them to attack Israel for no good cause; the same spirit that was in Haman that caused his hatred of the Jews of Persia is the same demonic spirit of anti-Semitism that continues to exist in the world today. I remember attending the Orthodox synagogue's Purim service during those tension-filled years. It seemed to me that as the people stirred up a thunderous noise, blotting out the name of Haman, they were actually and unknowingly doing spiritual warfare against this spirit of Amalek, which continues in its attempts to destroy Israel and the Jewish people. Many people underestimate the threat of Islam, thinking these terrorist bombings are only the unsupported, demented actions of a few extremists. Nothing could be further from the truth. Islam's goal is to destroy all who refuse to submit to the teachings of Muhammed. As such, it is a serious threat, not only to Jews, but to all peoples, especially those who hold true to the Bible and the God of Israel. Jews in Israel are not at war with Arabs, their cousins, but with the Spirit of Amalek, with Islam and its representatives today. Hamas, Islamic Jihad, Hizbullah, and

---

[1] David B. Goldberg, *'Esther, Pharaoh, Amalek, & Terrorist Bombings'*, Hashiva Quarterly, Volume XIX, No. 1, 1996-5756. A Friends of Zion Publication.

a dozen other Muslim terrorist groups are all funded by monies from Canada, European Union and the United States.[2]

Arafat and the P.L.O.

The P.L.O., formerly led by the late Yasser Arafat, despite their claims to want peace in the Middle East, actually support the terrorists. At the funeral of Yichyeh Ayash, the terrorist responsible for 51 Israeli deaths, Arafat proclaimed him a "martyr" and called on others to continue the jihad (holy war) i.e. terrorism. The Maoz Israel newsletter reports that Arafat's Fatah movement has republished their constitution (which is available on their web site). Instead of repudiating the section of the Palestinian covenant, which calls for Israel's annihilation, it re-affirms that the goal of the Palestinian people is to 'demolish' the Jewish state.[3]

More recently, the Barak government in the year 2000-2001, offered to hand over an astounding 98% of Judea and Samaria to the enemy. The Prime Minister also agreed to surrender some of our most holy, ancient sites, (some of which have already been completely destroyed by the Arabs who were supposed to protect them). In direct opposition to all of his election promises, Barak offered to divide Jerusalem, and to give the Palestinians sovereignty over the Temple Mount, all without the mandate of the Israeli Knesset (parliament) and over the protests of hundreds of thousands of Israeli demonstrators. All this has been offered for a supposed 'peace agreement', despite the Palestinians' non-compliance with the terms of the peace accords. A recent Jerusalem

---

[2] Note: This warning was written before the twin towers were destroyed by Muslim terrorists on Sept.11, 2001 in U.S.A.

[3] '*Maoz Israel Report*', chapter 1, article 19, September 1998.

Post[4] carried a front page headline, "WHY CAN'T 537 ISRAELIS VOTE IN THE UPCOMING ELECTIONS?" The answer is, of course, because they were murdered by Arab terrorists (since the Oslo "peace' agreement).

Jewish blood is being spilled like water today in the Land of Israel once again. Every 60 hours Arabs murder at least one Jew.

And yet Barak continued to negotiate with murderers and terrorists, promising to give away to Arafat practically all of our nations's historical and Biblical assets. More and more Israelis are saying, "Stop the killing! Enough of this intolerable slaughter. No more decimation of Jewish families." The only way the leaders of Israel can continue in this course of action, is due to ignorance of the Biblical record of our people such as in the Book of Esther and God's will for Israel. Sometimes it seems as if God is silent or hidden. But Purim teaches us that God is often found in that which is hidden and concealed.

What does God's Word have to say about the outcome of this terrorism? The Hebrew meaning of the name of one of the terrorist organizations, 'Hamas', is 'violence'. Notice that there is only one letter change between 'Hamas' and 'Haman'. A rabbi in Toronto, Canada, asked for a reaction to the attacks, replied: "As Isaiah prophesied (60:18), so we pray:

> **"Hamas (violence) shall no more be heard in our land, neither desolation, nor destruction within our borders; but our walls we shall call Yeshua[5], and Hallel (Praise) our gates."**

Amen

---

4 Feb 2, 2001, 9 Shvar 5761

5 The Hebrew word for salvation and name of our Saviour.

Foundation of Deception

Although the Palestinian Authority officially condemns terror attacks in their communications with the foreign media, presenting a front of peace to the world, they praise those same attacks in the official Palestinian Authority radio, TV and newspapers.

Even as Arafat basked in the media spotlight as "terrorist turned statesman", he told his audiences in Arabic that the negotiation process was merely a step in the direction of eventual victory. He repeatedly affirms that the P.L.O. would strategically use any territory obtained from Israel to pursue the ultimate aim: a state in the 'whole of "Palestine." The P.L.O. would therefore carry out the destruction of Israel in stages.[6] Most people do not understand that this kind of lying is a perfectly acceptable means to an end according to the tenets of Islam. According to al-Ghazali (1059-1111), one of the most important theologians and thinkers of Islam, lying is fully permissible in the war against the unbeliever: *"Know that the lie is not false in and of itself. When a lie is the only way to achieve a good result, it is permitted. Therefore we must lie if the truth would lead to an unpleasant outcome."*

On the same day that the 'Gaza-Jericho' First Agreement was signed on September 13, 1993, Jordanian TV showed a P.L.O. spokesman declaring, *"We are returning to 'Palestine.' Our flags will wave above Jerusalem, above the churches and mosques of Jerusalem."* [7]

Islam is a religion built on a foundation of deception and lies. Muhammad falsified the inheritance of Isaac, the father of Israel, onto Ishmael instead. He claimed that it was Ishmael, not Isaac, who was to be sacrificed, and is therefore the true heir. In doing

---

6 Patrick Goodenough, *'The Quest for Peace'*, Bikurei Tziyon (First Fruits of Zion, issue 68, Shemot/Exodus, Year 5761 (2001).

7 Herbert H. Nowitzky, *'Islam – The Religion & The Power'*, Hashivah

so, God's plan of redemption, from Abraham through Isaac, Jacob, Yehudah, and David, right up to Yeshua the Messiah, is annulled and irrelevant. The eternal chosenness of Israel is then transferred to the Arab nation, and the Jews are simply 'thieves' who have 'stolen' their land and their inheritance. In fact, God also gave wonderful promises to the descendants of Ishmael. True to God's Word, they have become a great nation and have inherited the blessing of vast amounts of oil-rich land. The land of Israel, and the lineage of the Messiah, however, belongs to the Jewish nation. God's covenant was established with Isaac.

> **"And Abraham said to God, 'If only Ishmael might live under your blessing!' Then God said, 'Yes, but your wife Sarah will bear you a son, and you will call him <u>Isaac (Yitzchak). I will establish my covenant with him as an everlasting covenant for his descendants after him.</u> And as for Ishmael, I have heard you: I will surely bless him: I will make him fruitful and will greatly increase his numbers. He will be the father of twelve rulers, and I will make him into a (great) nation. <u>But my covenant</u> I will establish with Isaac...'"** (Gen. 17:18-21)

Note: In the Hebrew, God uses the words 'goy gadol', which is translated in most Bibles as 'great nation'. In fact, the word 'gadol' usually means 'big or large', but is also used for 'great'. No one can deny that today, the descendants of Ishmael, the Arabic nations, are fruitful in numbers of people, and also big or large in size of land area, but great? This is a subjective judgment. Do our Bibles contain a built-in bias?

God Issues A Warning

What dire warning does God issue to those who boast against Israel; who disregard God's covenant with Israel through Isaac and attempt to gain possession of the land for themselves?

> "Because you have said, "These two nations and countries will be ours and we will take possession of them," even though I the Lord was there, therefore as surely as I live, declares the Sovereign Lord, I will treat you in accordance with the anger and jealousy you showed in your hatred of them and I will make myself known among them when I judge you. Then you will know that I the Lord have heard all the contemptible things you have said against the mountains of Israel. You said, "They have been laid waste and have been given over to us to devour." You boasted against me and spoke against me without restraint, and I heard it. This is what the Sovereign Lord says: While the whole earth rejoices, I will make you desolate. Because you rejoiced when the inheritance of the house of Israel became desolate, that is how I will treat you. You will be desolate, O Mount Seir, you and all of Edom. Then they will know that I am the Lord." (Ezek. 35:10-15)

Understand that 'Edom' (from the Hebrew Adom, meaning 'red'), stands for Esau and his descendants. The other name for Esau was Adom because he was born red and hairy. His descendants settled in the mountains of Seir, which corresponds to areas of

Jordan today.[8] The chapters in Ezekiel (35-39) are especially significant for the time period in which we now live, after the rebirth of the nation of Israel. They give us an eye into the future to understand the plan of God. We need to heed the warnings of the Lord, know His position, and warn those who have not heard or understood. Many Muslims do not have possession of a Bible and do not know that they are in grave danger in opposing God and His people Israel.

Facts & Myths About Israel and the Palestinians

The Facts

- An Islamic people known as the Palestinians do not have original claim to the Land of Israel.
- Israel became a nation by divine decree in 1312 B.C.E., 2000 years before the rise of Islam.
- The Palestinians did not have a continuous presence in the Land of Israel.
- The Romans applied the name "Palestine from Phillistine" to the Land of Israel in an attempt to obliterate the Jewish connection to Zion.
- The Jews have had a continuous presence in the Land for 3,000 years.
- The Jewish Bible mentions Jerusalem *over 700 times.*
- The Koran says nothing about Jerusalem.
- It mentions Mecca hundreds of times and Medina countless times, but never mentions Jerusalem even once.

---

8 For an excellent explanation of Edom, and the Palestinian issue from a Biblical perspective, I recommend to you a book by Norma Archibald, *'The Mountains of Israel, The West Bank and the Bible',*

- Palestine has never existed as an autonomous entity.
- There has never been a land known as Palestine governed by Palestinians.
- There is no language known as Palestinian. There is no distinct Palestinian culture.
- Palestinians are Arabs, indistinguishable from Jordanians, Syrians, Lebanese, Iraqis, etc.
- The Arabs control 99.9% of the Middle East lands.
- Israel represents one tenth of one percent of the land mass.[9]

Suicide Warriors Pretty in Pink

I can understand Bible-ignorant people of the world being deceived about these issues. What really perplexes me, however, is how Christians who (I assume) read God's Word can be siding with the enemies of Israel. Unfortunately, some Christians (even the very elect) are also being deceived into supporting the Palestinian cause, totally unaware that they are placing themselves in position against God Himself! Christian TV-station empire with $100 million in annual revenues, has built TV stations in eastern Jerusalem, Jericho and Ramallah for the Palestinians (with deals signed to build others in Bethlehem, Gaza and Hebron). In their newsletters they no longer write about Israel, other than mentioning what they call Israeli military brutality; it's simply the "Holy Land." They are spending hundreds of thousands of dollars hoping to beam the gospel into Arab homes.[10] Instead, this money is being used to project anti-Semitic programming into thousands of Palestinian homes daily. These programs incite violence against

---

9 *'The Jerusalem Post'*, Friday, February 2, 2001, pg. A7
10 *'Can Christians & Jews Achieve Peace with the Muslims?'* Special Issue by David B. Goldberg, "Hashivah" – The Return.

the people of Israel and passionately call for Jihad (Holy War) to rid 'their land' of the Israeli presence and 'liberate' Jerusalem!

Special programs are specifically targeted for children to indoctrinate them, even at a tender age into hatred against the Jewish people. On one such program, a little girl in a pretty, pink dress with puffy sleeves, sings about how she longs to be a suicide bomber when she grows up so that she can give her life for her country and for Allah. While she sings, Mickey Mouse and other Disney characters prance about on stage.

Note: On September 5th, 1999, three terrorists blew themselves up in terrorist attacks in Haifa and Tiberias. Only the grace and protection of the Almighty God prevented a greater loss of life. The terrorists planned to plant the bombs on crowded buses, but 'forgot' about the time change of an hour and ended up only killing themselves. Who were the suicide bombers? For the first time, they were Israeli Arab citizens! Since this time, Arab violence against Jews has escalated; many of the perpetrators are Arab-Israelis who enjoy all the privileges and benefits of an Israeli citizen, and yet they attempt to destroy the nation and its people.

I recently received report of a Canadian rural denominational church that had taken upon themselves the task of giving relief to Palestinians whom apparently had their illegally built homes bulldozed by Israelis. The members of this church, in their misguided zeal and misinformation, have developed hatred towards the Israelis themselves. The Word of God tells us that in the last days, many people will be deceived, even the very elect. The following is a pro-Palestinian anti-Israel message taken from a dialog with the Church of Scotland, after someone wrote them to ask why they openly support Palestinian causes, in light of what the Scripture teaches about Israel

From: David Sinclair,
Church and Nation Secretary, Church of Scotland

> "We have looked at both sides and, having done so, take the view that, while there are many people of good will, nevertheless the cry for justice is to be heard overwhelmingly from the Palestinians. If Israel wants to be a holy people then it must behave differently, it must become what G-d wants it to be. Until then it cannot expect to be judged any differently from others who oppress their neighbors."

We must stay rooted and grounded in God's word for the Truth. Every mature Bible Believer is engaged in a spiritual battle, even involuntarily, with this spirit of Amalek, manifested in the false religion of Islam.

Islam And World Unity

Many Christians, and Jews believe that Allah is the same God that they revere – the one, true God. This, however, is also a deception. The revelations of Muhammad (570-632), founder of Islam, were recorded in the Quran (or Koran). At the time that Muhammad preached publicly in his hometown of Mecca in 610, more than 360 deities were worshipped there. A giant black stone, Kaaba, formed the physical center of the pagan idolatry. Today, every practicing Muslim's central desire is a pilgrimage (hajj) to the Kaaba in Mecca. Muhammad, who learned about faith in a single, invisible God from Jews and Christians, elevated one pagan deity, Allah, as the one God and rejected the other deities of Mecca. 'Allah', therefore, contrary to popular belief, cannot be translated as 'God'. I was dumbfounded to discover at a 'reconciliation' conference attended by Messianic Jews and Palestinian Christians recently in Jerusalem, the people singing, not only praise and worship to Adonai, Yeshua, but also to Allah! At this same 'ecumenical retreat center', the bookstore displayed and sold the book, 'The Palestinian Liberation Manifesto'. *"The fundamental goal of Islam is the creation of a united society of all peoples and all nations under Islamic rule… Jihad, holy war (including acts of terrorism and suicide-bombings), is the means to that end…"* [11]

Beware of the deceptive and seductive language of the ecumenical movement – of world unity, love, harmony and peace amongst all peoples of the world. There will be peace on earth one day, but this will only be achieved through the government of the Prince of Peace, not through the Pope shaking hands with Jewish and Muslim leaders.

> **"For to us a child is born, to us a son is given, and the government will be on his shoulders. And he will be called Wonderful Counselor, Mighty Good, Everlasting Father, Prince of Peace. Of the increase of his government and peace there will be no end. He will reign on David's throne and over his kingdom, establishing and upholding it with justice and righteousness from that time on and forever. The zeal of the Lord almighty will accomplish this."** (Is. 9:6-7)

When will this be accomplished? When the Lord returns to defeat the enemies of Israel and to set up His kingdom in Jerusalem. Indeed, the Messiah, from the tribe of Judah, will one day rule from the throne of King David, and Jerusalem will be the

---

[11] Herbert H. Nowtzky, *'The Quran & Jihad – Holy War'*

capital, not only of Israel, but of the world.

> "At that time they shall call Jerusalem the throne of the Lord, and all the nations shall be gathered unto it, to the name of the Lord, to Jerusalem; neither shall they walk any more after the imagination of their evil heart." (Jer. 3:17)

CHAPTER THREE

A JEW IS TAKING OVER THE WORLD

Much of the anti-Semitism in the world centers around the belief that Jews are united in a conspiracy to take over the world. I had a dear, older lady stand in front of me at my Judaica and book display table at a summer Christian camp and tell me, in all sincerity, that the Jews are taking over all the banks of the world. In a sense, there is a kernel of truth to these beliefs. One day, a Jew, Yeshua the Messiah, is going to take over the world! There is no other way.

> **"Then the Lord will go out and fight against those nations, as he fights in the day of battle. On that day his feet will stand on the Mount of Olives, east of Jerusalem,...The Lord will be king over the whole earth. On that day there will be one Lord, and his name the only name."** (Zech. 14:3, 4, 9)

Jewish people sing these prophetic words every Sabbath,

> "Bayom Hahu, Bayom Hahu, Y'hye Adonai echad; U'shmo, u'shmo, u'shmo echad."

(On that day, there will be one Adonai, and his name will be one.)

One day this Word will come to pass. This should be good news for those who believe in and are devoted to the God of Israel, the God of Abraham, Isaac, and Jacob.

Israel will be the leader amongst the nations and whatever nation will not serve her will perish. These are not my own vain imaginings, but the prophetic Word of God.

> **"For the nation and kingdom which will not serve you shall perish, and those nations shall be utterly ruined."** (Is. 60:12)

It is incredible how the adversary of God and His people twists the Biblical prophecies in order to stir up anti-Semitism. Recently, a demonic tool used to fertilize the seeds of anti-Semitism in the nations reared its ugly head again. The 'Protocols of the Elders of Zion',[1] an anti-Semitic fabrication which was not composed by any 'elders' and does not come from 'Zion' is being distributed once again. This is despite corroborating court decisions around the globe which have all concluded that it is a work of forgery and plagiarism, composed of fictitious notes describing how the Jews are supposedly conspiring to take over the world and subjugate it under a '*King from Zion.*'

> "In Japan, the Protocols have been distributed among the people in large quantities for some years. More than 60 editions have been published

---

[1] Originally the Protocols were put together by the Illuminati and were "of the Elders of Sion" not to be confused with Zion. They were and are an accurate blueprint of the plan for world government by 'The Order', not Zionists. Sion is an occult group.

in Arab nations. In bookstores in Cairo and in other Muslim capitals, this anti-Semitic forgery is a best seller. In Saudi Arabia, every visiting foreign dignitary, whether from the field of politics, religion or business receives a special, artistic edition as a momento."[2]

This is perhaps understandable, as these people openly proclaim themselves enemies of Israel and the Jews, but Christians? Unfortunately, they too are also being misled.

Christians Also Misled

Dr. Goldberg, in his article, describes how a Jewish proofreader, whose family attended a Christian church, discovered that a famous evangelical church in Toronto, Canada, had given a local printing firm a job to publish the Protocols. He approached the ministers of the church to persuade them to refrain from distributing this libelous book, but was gruffly rebuffed and sent away. Dr. Goldberg's son discovered the Protocols and other anti-Semitic materials being sold in a Christian bookstore in North Hollywood, California, alongside their Bibles and gospel music albums. The shopkeeper said, in an undertone, that he carried a book which 'revealed that Christian children are murdered by the Jews in Chicago every year, and their blood is used for the Passover meal.' This man described himself as a 'born again Christian'.[15] An American Charismatic Baptist church in Indiana distributes pamphlets containing anti-Semitic statements, false accusations against the Jews, and publicizes the Protocols of the Elders of Zion as authentic. Ironically, the author states that other

---

2 Dr. Herbert Goldberg, *'The "Protocols of the Elders of Zion" Unmasked!',* "Hashivah" – The Return, Volume XVII, Number 2, 1994-5754

pamphlets distributed by this church deal with deliverance and teach the reader how to drive out demons. *"It seems, though,"* says Goldberg, *"that this congregation has not yet driven the demon of lies and of anti-Semitism out from its midst."*

God is not mocked; He will not tolerate this situation forever. Why do people, even Christians, persist in believing and perpetuating these lies from the enemy? Is it possible they love darkness more than the light? We know that the truth will set us free. I believe that each person who knows the truth has a responsibility to share it with others.

Anti-Semitism North-American Style

Today, we are experiencing a worldwide rise in anti-Semitism once again. Even in the United States, we see the ugly face of anti-Semitism re-appearing. In 1999, three synagogues in Sacramento, California were firebombed, a man went on a shooting rampage against Orthodox Jews walking home from a Chicago synagogue, and another man walked into a Jewish Community Center (J.C.C.) in Los Angeles, opening fire on the children, wounding several of them. The Chicago suspect, Benjamin Nathaniel Smith, was a member of the World Church of the Creator, a white supremacist organization. According to the Simon Wiesenthal Center, which monitors the world for anti-Semitism, this Church has a major presence on the Internet to spread their classic anti-Semitic lies about the "Jewish-controlled media" and the "Jewish controlled government". Smith shot and killed himself after a police chase, and was found to have tattooed across his chest, 'Sabbath Breaker'. Here is some of the fruit that comes with defiance of the laws of God, and people belonging to a church so divorced from its Jewish roots that it sees the Jews as the 'enemy'.

As I studied the black and white newsprint photo of police leading a whole string of young children to safety outside the J.C.C.'s gates, tears came suddenly and unexpectedly to my eyes. My youngest son is about the same age as these children. How must these tender ones that the Lord loves so much feel about some stranger bursting into their 'safe place' and shooting their friends with real bullets, just because they are of Jewish descent? The assailant, 37 year-old white supremacist Buford O'Neal Furrow, smiled up at the camera with obvious delight in his deed. He declared this shooting, *"a wake up call to America to start killing Jews."*

The fall season, at which time this attack occurred, is the time for the blowing of the shofar – as a kind of 'wake up' call. The prophet Jeremiah speaks of a time in the latter days when the Jewish people would turn from their ways and come back to the Lord and to the land of Israel. This period of re-gathering will not be without trial and tribulation for God's people, however. First will come the fishers, attempting to lure the Jewish people out of Exile before 'the hunters' arrive. (Jer 16:16)

> "Indeed, this is a bitter-sweet season of wake-up calls: to the Jew-hunter to come out, for the Jew to go home, and for the Christian to take a stand."[3]

We cannot think that North America and Western European countries are too civilized to engage in this kind of filth. Nine days after the L.A. rampage, the police force discovered several containers filled with medical waste marked with swastikas and anti-Semitic messages. On one container a picture of Furrow O'Neal was found. Norwalk Mayor Frank Esposito reported to Associated Press, *"I don't even know how to even begin describing the ignorance...I don't know where our mentality's going."* [4]

---

3 From the Editor's Desk: *'The Season for Wake-Up Calls is Upon Us: Will We Perceive it?'*, The Call of the Shofar, Sept. 99, pg.7
4 *Ibid.*

Yes, somehow we can accept the rising anti-Semitism in a country like Russia. In a recent report from 'Prayer for Israel', I heard that posters in areas of the former Soviet Union encourage their citizens to 'rid Russia of all Jews' and even give a telephone number people can call to obtain a weapon for this purpose. Russia – understandable due to its history, but America? We may recall from the not too distant past, however, that Germany, prior to WW II was also a civilized, Christian, democratic nation. Many of the German Jews were assimilated into German society and culture, holding positions of prominence in educational, governmental, financial, medical, and other fields of endeavor. And we know the tragic end of the story for the European Jewry.

Esther and Exile

Perhaps we can gain some insights into our current day situation from the wisdom of the Bible. In the book of Esther, the Jews were Persian, living outside the land of promise, Israel, even though the Persian King, Cyrus, had given permission for the Jews to return home. Perhaps they didn't want to give up their businesses, homes, and perceived security to venture into an unknown future in a country that after such a long exile seemed 'foreign'. We can see that even though the Persian Jews were well-integrated into society and seemingly secure, it only took one anti-Semite coming to power to threaten their entire existence, just as happened in Germany in World War II. We can discover several parallels between pre-WW II Germany and conditions in the world today: threat of economic collapse, loss of faith in governments, lawlessness, increase in crime and violence, and the denial of God along with the deification of man (rise in New Age religion and philosophies). A major, global crisis could usher in martial law, dictatorial governmental control, and the demonically inspired 'New World Order'. This corresponds with the Bible's predictions of a world ruler who will persecute the people of God and wage war against the Kingdom of God.

Responsibility of the Church

Today, anti-Semitism is rising, especially in the Slavic countries; but even in North America where most Jews feel very safe and secure, it only takes one Haman, one Hitler, to come to power. Christians need to stop listening to the media and start listening to God, encouraging and helping Jewish people in returning to Israel, the land of promise and refuge. Because of the language barrier, culture shock, and financial hardship, the struggle can be so intense that some people are driven back into exile[5], contrary to the Word of God.

> **"I will plant them in this land assuredly with my whole heart and with my whole soul."** (Jer. 32:41)

Satan wants to prove God a liar by uprooting as many of the returning exiles as possible. The Bible says that it is the Gentiles who will help the Jews get back to their own land and that there they will live securely.

> **"See, I will beckon to the Gentiles, I will lift up my banner to the peoples; they will bring your sons in their arms and carry your daughters on their shoulders."** (Is. 49:22)

There are Jewish people who need financial as well as

---

[5] In 2005, our family returned to Canada due to religious persecution. Because of our faith in Yeshua, the Jewish Messiah, David was denied a visa to work or live in Israel. (see note)

prayer support to become successfully transplanted back into their homeland. I know that it is God who brought us home to this beautiful land of Israel, but He used the faithful prayers as well as generous financial support of Gentile Christians in order to accomplish His will. For this we will always be grateful. Paul clearly exhorts Gentile Christians regarding this duty and responsibility towards the Jews, especially the 'saints in Jerusalem' – Jewish believers:

> **"For if the Gentiles have shared in the Jews' spiritual blessings, they owe it to the Jews to share with them their material blessings."** (Rom. 15:27)

What worth can we place upon the Bible, the Messiah, and a place in an everlasting covenant with God all received through the Jewish people? By sharing their material blessings, Christians can play a part in helping to fulfill God's mandate to resettle His people back into their own land.

> **"And I will plant them upon their land, and they shall no more be plucked up out of their land which I have given them, says the Lord your God."** (Amos 9:15)

Ed Warmoth, Project Shofar's Christian Branch President states, *"We Christians in particular owe our Spiritual heritage to the sons and daughters of Jacob. Today is the day to fulfill our obligation to be a strong support to our Jewish brethren – both spiritually and physically. It is not enough to simply pray for the peace of Jerusalem."*

He Who Keepeth Israel
Neither Slumbers Nor Sleeps

What will happen to all the Jewish people who remain in exile at this time?

We also see in the story of Esther that even though the Persian Jews were probably not in God's perfect will and timing by remaining in Persia, refusing to return to the land of promise open to them, God remained faithful. He is still watching over and protecting His people.

> **"He who watches over Israel neither slumbers nor sleeps."** (Ps. 121:4)

The way of return was open to all Jews again in 1948, but many are content to live in their lands of exile, even though this was part of a curse. *"The Jewish people were never meant to find peace and tranquility outside of our Homeland. We were scattered to the four corners of the world as a punishment."* [6]

In spite of the increasing evidence of anti-Semitism, America is booming; many Israelis and Russian Jews are trying to immigrate to the States or Canada. Why would anyone want to leave this supposed North American 'land of milk and honey' to immigrate to Israel, where it can be such a struggle to survive? When people found out that we were new olim (new immigrants) from Canada, they just stared at us and shook their heads, as if to say, 'Must be meshuganah' (crazy). This oddity factor and their curiosity sometimes open doors to share Biblical prophecy. Just as modern prophets such as Theodore Herzl tried to warn the Jews of Europe to flee the Diaspora before it consumed them, today's prophets

---

[6] America too is part of the 'cursed exile', Gary M. Cooperberg, *'The Call of the Shofar'*, Vol 2 Issue 2, September 1999.

are issuing this same warning to North American Jews. A terrible loss of life is being predicted.[7] *"Here, in comfortable America, the land of liberty, flames of hate are inching ever closer to the heels of G-d's Chosen People' so much so, that even the baffled local and national authorities have admitted that they are having trouble putting out all of the fires."* [8]

Unfortunately, as it was then, so it is now, most will not listen until it is too late. I vividly recall having lunch with a man who survived the holocaust. I remained glued to my chair as he retold the story of how he narrowly escaped the Polish ghetto where his entire family perished. Even after fifty years, he still wept as he remembered having to leave his mother behind, never to see her again. The one question that burned in my mind was, 'Why didn't more escape with you?' There seemed to be ample opportunity at that time for others to flee. His answer was that most of them did not want to break up their families. Also, they were optimistic – they never imagined that it would actually get that bad. The sad part about this is that, although this man survived because he thought for himself and faced reality, a thriving business and family considerations now prevent him from seriously considering making the move back to the land of Israel. When I tell him that the signs of the times indicate we may be entering another such period, he says,

"Oh, I'm optimistic; I don't think it will ever get that bad."
God warns us not to trust in riches but in Him.

"Riches certainly make themselves wings; they fly away as an eagle toward heaven." (Prov. 23:5)

---

7   Tom Hess, *'Let My People Go'*, (Progressive Vision, Washington, D.C.)
8   *'The Season for Wake-Up Calls is Upon Us: Will We Perceive It?"*, from the Editor's desk, 'The Call of the Shofar', Sept. 99.

David Wilkerson has recently written a book in which he predicts God's swift and certain judgment upon North America through a sudden financial crash.[9] Wilkerson says: *"The American dream is going to turn into the American nightmare. It will occur suddenly – without warning – and no one will be able to explain how or why it happened. There will be sellers only – no buyers."*

Whenever the economy of a nation falls, the Jews seem to get the blame and anti-Semitic persecution increases. Why? I'm not sure. Perhaps this 'joke' I heard expresses the sentiment:

"Did you hear that the Jew, Goldberg, was responsible for the sinking of the Titanic?"

"I thought it was an iceberg."

"Goldberg, Sternberg, Iceberg, what's the difference?"

Let us pray for the liberty of many Jewish people – that God will bring them home before it is too late. It is possible that we may have very little time left. We also need to pray for the protection of the Jewish people who will be left behind due to their own unwillingness to move in response to the warnings of modern day prophets. Even in Persian Exile under threat of annihilation from Haman, God still protected and delivered His people.

Judgement on the gods of Egypt

God also promises that He will bring His people out of exile from all the four directions – including the West.

> **"I have spoken it; I will also bring it to pass. I have purposed it; I will also do it."** (Is. 46:11)

---

9 *America's Last Call – On the Brink of a Financial Holocaust',* (Wilkerson Trust Publications, Lindale Texas, 1998).

If it is the god of materialism keeping the North American Jews in bondage, then the Lord, Yehovah our God, will bring down this false god, just as He defeated the false gods of Egypt.

> **"I will bring judgment on all the gods of Egypt."**
> (Ex. 12:12)

God will deliver His people from their North American Egypt, just as He once did from ancient Egypt.

> **"I will redeem you with an outstretched arm and with mighty acts of judgment. I will take you as my own people I will be your God. Then you will know that I am the Lord your God who brought you out from under the yoke of the Egyptians. And I will bring you to the land I swore with uplifted hand to give to Abraham, to Isaac and to Jacob. I will give it to you as a possession. I am Yehovah יהוה."** (Ex. 6:6-9)

Do you realize that God actually lifted his hand in holy oath to give the land of Israel to Abraham, Isaac (not Ishmael) and to Jacob's (not Esau's) descendants? This is the same portion of land that today, the Israeli government, under pressure from America and the world is preparing to hand over possession to Ishmael and Esau's descendants? And yet, God has a plan for today. The prophets tell us that this 'Second Exodus' will be even a greater miracle, a greater deliverance than the first under Moses.

The Second Exodus

> "Therefore, behold, the days are coming," says the Lord, "that they shall no longer say, 'As the Lord lives who brought up the children of Israel from the land of Egypt,' but, 'As the Lord lives who brought up and led the descendants of the house of Israel from the north country and from all the countries where I had driven them. And they shall dwell in their own land." (Jer. 23:7-8)

How exactly will this be accomplished? Only the one who will lead them really knows.

> "Behold the days are coming," says the Lord, "That I will raise to David a Branch of righteousness; A King shall reign and prosper, And execute judgment and righteousness in the earth. In His days Judah will be saved, and Israel will dwell safely; now this is His name by which He will be called: ADONAI OUR RIGHTEOUSNESS (יהוה TZIDKEINU). (Jer. 23:5-6)

This is the long awaited King Moshiach, the true Messiah, who carries the name, honor and glory of Yehovah our God. This is the one for whom Jewish people have affirmed as a foundation of faith, 'I believe in the coming of the Messiah, though he tarry, yet will I wait.' He will redeem them, judge them, bring them into covenant with Him, and bring some of them to dwell in the land of Israel, even if it takes the hand of His fury (some devastating catastrophe) to do it.

> "What you have in your mind shall never be, when you say, 'we will be like the Gentiles, like the families in other countries, serving wood and stone.'" (Ezek. 20:32)

Weren't the German Jews prior to WWII highly assimilated? Don't most Jewish people in the nations want to live just like the Gentiles? But this will never be. God has preserved the Jewish nations and will continue to preserve them as a called out, Holy people. The good news is that anyone may now join them – be grafted in to the olive tree and be nourished by the same root (providing they agree to live by God's requirements).

> "As I live," says the Lord God, "surely with a mighty hand and an outstretched arm and with fury poured out, I will rule over you. I will bring you out from the peoples and gather you out of the countries where you are scattered, with a mighty hand and an outstretched arm and with fury poured out. I will bring you into the wilderness of the peoples and there I will judge you face to face. Just as I judged your fathers in the desert of the land of Egypt, so I will judge you, declares Adonai Yehovah. I will make you pass under the rod, and I will bring you into the bond of the covenant. I will purge the rebels from among you, and those who transgress against me. I will bring them out of the country where they dwell, but they will not enter the land of Israel. Then you will know that I am Yehovah." (Ezek. 20:33-38)

CHAPTER FOUR

THE ARM OF THE LORD

It is the 'Arm of the Lord', the Messiah Yeshua, who will judge the nations and rule. It is He, and not some foreign, Gentile god upon whom God's people will finally put their trust for salvation.

> "Behold, Adonai Yehovah shall come with a strong hand, and HIS ARM shall rule for Him;" (Isa. 40:10)

> "And MY ARM will judge the peoples; the coastlands will wait upon Me, and on MY ARM they will trust.... (Isa. 51:5)

> "Awake, awake, put on strength, O ARM OF THE LORD! Awake as in the ancient days, in the generations of old...so the ransomed of the Lord shall return, and come to Zion with singing, with everlasting joy on their heads. They shall obtain joy and gladness; Sorrow and sighing shall flee away." (Is. 51:5, 9, 11)

> "Yehovah has made bare HIS HOLY ARM in the eyes of all the nations; and all the ends of the earth shall see the salvation (Yeshua) of our God (Eloheinu)." (Is. 52:10)

Yes, the hour is short; the day is coming soon when God will reveal His Holy Arm to all of mankind. The Jewish people also will know Him as the Lamb who was slain – the One who poured out His soul unto death in order to make atonement for our sin.

Isaiah 53 – King Messiah

> *"Who has believed our report?*
> *And to whom has the ARM OF*
> *THE LORD been revealed?*
> *Surely He has borne our griefs*
> *and carried our sorrows;*
> *But He was wounded*
> *for our transgressions,*
> *He was bruised for our iniquities;*
> *The chastisement for our peace*
> *was upon Him,*
> *and by His stripes we are healed.*
> *All we like sheep have gone astray;*
> *we have turned, every one,*
> *to his own way;*
> *and the Lord has laid on Him*
> *the iniquity of us all.*
> *He was led as a lamb*
> *to the slaughter...*
> *For He was cut off from*
> *the land of the living;*
> *for the transgressions of*
> *my people He was stricken*
> *because He poured out His soul*
> *unto death and He was numbered*
> *with the transgressors,*
> *and He bore the sin of many,*
> *and made intercession*
> *for the transgressors."* (Is. 53)

The Arm of the Lord

The arm of the Lord, the Messiah, Yeshua, is the perfect picture of the Azazel, the scapegoat, upon whom the Cohen Hagadol (High Priest) laid all the sins of Israel on the Day of Atonement. Yeshua is the perfect kippur (atonement), because He, alone, was without sin. Only His blood, sacrificed out of incomprehensible love for us, can purify us and cleanse us from our sins.

> **"Though your sins are like scarlet, they shall be as white as snow."** (Is. 1:18)

Now that the anti-Missionary movements are becoming more active and organized - publishing and distributing anti-Yeshua materials, they are teaching Jewish people that Isaiah 53 does not speak of the Messiah, but of the nation of Israel. The early Rabbinical authorities came to an agreement that these scriptures indeed speak of the Messiah. *"Our rabbis with one voice accept and affirm the opinion that the prophet is speaking of the King Messiah, and we shall ourselves also adhere to the same view."* [1]

This crucial prophetic chapter of scripture has been effectively hidden from Jewish eyes for a period of time. It is omitted from the weekly Sabbath readings (parashot), and considered forbidden to read by most Rabbincal authorities who focus on the Talmud, which was written by men, rather than the Torah, which is of divine origin. But one day, God will pour out His Spirit upon His people and remove the blindness from their eyes and they will see and recognize Him.

> **"They will look on me, the one they have pierced, and they will mourn for him as one mourns for an only child, and grieve bitterly for him as one grieves for a firstborn son."** (Zech. 12:10)

---

[1] Rabbi Moses Alshech, *'Good News, The Magazine with a Message'*, Special Rabbis' Edition, (P.O. Box 7848, Johannesburg, 2000, South Africa).

When will this take place? When that spirit of Amalek rises once again to destroy Israel. When all the nations of the earth are gathered against Jerusalem. When all seems to be lost.

> "On that day, when all the nations of the earth are gathered against her, I will make Jerusalem an immovable rock for all the nations. All who try to move it will injure themselves...On that day I will set out to destroy all the nations that attack Jerusalem." (Zech. 12:3, 9)

What Will God Do?

This battle is the Lord's. As Purim proves, the Jewish people are not simply at the mercy of those who hate them. God has something to say about the fate of the Jewish people:

> "But you, Israel, are My servant, Jacob whom I have chosen, The descendants of Abraham My friend. You whom I have taken from the ends of the earth, and called from its farthest region, and said to you, 'You are My servant, I have chosen you and have not cast you away: Fear not, for I am with you; Be not dismayed, for I am your God. I will strengthen you, Yes, I will help you, I will uphold you with My righteous right hand." (Is. 41:8-10)

and of her enemies:

> "Behold, all those who were incensed against you shall be ashamed and disgraced; they shall be as nothing, and those who strive with you shall perish. You shall seek them and not find them – those who contended with you. Those who war against you

> shall be as nothing, as a nonexistent thing. For I, the Lord your God, will hold your right hand, saying to you, "Fear not, I will help you." "Fear not, you worm Jacob, You men of Israel! I will help you," says the Lord and your Redeemer, the Holy One of Israel." (Is. 41:11-14)

Now we know that God does not waste words; if He chooses to repeat Himself, this is a crucial word to His people. Fear not, I will help you. Fear not, I will help you. Your enemies will be as if they had never existed. Even the memory of Amalek will be blotted out from under heaven.

I Will Bless Those Who Bless You...

God is not mentioned even once in the book of Esther, but He is always behind the scenes! A biblical principle that proves itself relevant throughout history and even up until this day is that God blesses those who bless His people and curses those who curse them (Gen. 12:3). The gallows that Haman built on which to hang Mordecai were the same gallows that he himself was hung on. God reversed the curses back onto those who dare to curse His treasure. In Deuteronomy chapter 30, God speaks of the time that He will re-gather the children of Israel to the land. He also makes several promises, one of which is a reversal of the curse:

> "The Lord your God will put all these curses on your enemies who hate and persecute you." (Deut. 30: 7)

God speaks of judgment upon Edom and calls them

> "The people of My curse." (Is. 34:5)

Why has God cursed Edom? It is because they have cursed and not blessed the Jews.

God clearly promises to ally Himself with Abraham, thereby blessing anyone who blesses him and cursing anyone who curses him. In a sense, God puts his arm around Abraham and says 'whoever is your friend is my friend, but whoever comes against you – they'll have to deal with me!" In the movie, 'The Bear', a wonderful scene shows a vulnerable, weak, baby bear scrapping with a cougar. The cougar moves with threatening snarls on the offensive against the frightened bear. Trying to appear big and fierce, he stands up on his two hind legs and gives a tiny roar. Suddenly, the cougar startles, turns tail and runs away. The little bear is so pleased with himself, thinking proudly of how he scared off a ferocious cougar all on his own. It is then that the camera changes focus to show the form of an enormous male Grizzly Bear standing up on his two hind legs directly behind the smaller form of the wee warrior. This is such a wonderful picture of God fighting our battles for us.

Be Careful How You Touch the Apple of God's Eye

For the people of Israel, God gives a comforting promise, and for their enemies, a dire warning.

> **"For whoever touches you, touches the apple of his eye."** (Zech. 2:8)

The 'apple of the eye' is the pupil, the most sensitive part of an exquisitely sensitive part of the body. I don't know about you, but I certainly would not want to be poking my fingers into the pupil of God Almighty's eyeball. In fact, I feel sorry for anyone who would attempt this foolish act. History has borne out the validity and continuity of this principal for Abraham's seed, the Jewish people. Pharaoh and the Egyptian oppressors who ordered all Hebrew babies cast into the Nile, were themselves drowned in the Sea of Reeds. He, who plotted the destruction of the Jews in Persia, ended his life on the very same gallows he built for Mordechai the Jew. Even Haman's wife knew this divine principal and said,

> "Since Mordecai, before whom your downfall has started, is of Jewish origin, you cannot stand against him – you will surely come to ruin!" (Esth. 6:13)

(Oh, that more men would listen to the wisdom that proceeds from the lips of their wives! ☺)

Those who bless Israel are blessed and those who curse Israel are definitely cursed. This principal is still in effect today.

Curse vs. Curse

In the Hebrew, two different words are used for curse in Gen. 12:3. 'I will curse' is 'Aor" אאר, derived from the similar word, 'Aroor' ארור used when God cursed the serpent in the Garden of Eden (Gen.3:14). However, for 'whoever curses you', the word is 'm'kalelcha' מקללך derived from the root kalal קלל. As well as 'curse', kalal can mean to blaspheme, treat with contempt or disdain, despise, or even to treat lightly or not to take seriously. I believe this is a serious issue, especially in the Christian community, which needs to be addressed. God, by His own words, has called down a curse upon all those who treat Abraham's seed with anything less than proper respect and dignity. This, therefore, refers not only to active 'cursing' of the Jews, but also the attitude of our hearts, which may manifest in anti-Jewish 'humor' and comments.

Cursing in the Church

In speaking in some churches on this subject, I have seen two reactions in people. In one, the person with contempt for Jewish people in their own heart or in their ancestral lineage repents and allows the Holy Spirit to cleanse them of this sin of anti-Semitism and give them a clean heart and renew a right spirit within them. In the other, the person stubbornly remains in sinful arrogance and pride, or else denies the validity of this divine curse. At one particular meeting in a large, Pentecostal, German church I presented the Messiah in the Passover. One precious man called me later, and with a broken and contrite spirit, confessed the sins of his father and grandfather who had been Nazis, and his own anti-Semitic attitude. He explained that during the presentation, when the Word of God came forth, he felt all traces of this contempt for Jewish people drain out of him through his feet and into the floor. (Probably heading back to the pit from which it came). Later, I found out that a call came to the Jewish Community Center from a man whose family was Nazi; he was letting them know that he had changed his will to include the J.C.C. as benefactors. This is truly faith accompanied by deeds and it served as a witness to my father who relayed the incident. Talk is cheap; we must demonstrate the fruit of repentance.

At the same time that some were touched by the cleansing power of the Holy Spirit, however, others remained hard-hearted. My teenage daughter happened to be caring for my youngest son in the nursery while I was speaking on Passover in this same church. Everyone in the nursery could hear the message piped in through speakers, and some of the women proceeded to mock both the message and the Jewish people. My daughter graciously but pointedly said to her little brother:

"You will have to wait to see MOMMY when MOMMY has finished speaking."

She exited, leaving an embarrassed silence in the air, and

hopefully some red-faced women seriously considering their words. Even if my daughter had not overheard their reviling of the Jews, God certainly hears and knows all, even that which is hidden in the secret places of our hearts. He is faithful and just to forgive us our sins, and to cleanse us from all unrighteousness. Why should we keep this sin under cover when we can renounce it and find forgiveness and freedom from the curse that may have been resting upon us for our reviling of Abraham's seed.

One woman admitted to the sin of anti-Semitism in her family, but then claimed that it was 'no big deal', since 'they didn't really curse the Jews'. We can see from the words God uses that there is more to this issue than simply 'not really cursing'.

The Rise of Anti-Semitism in the Church

God can take anything meant for evil and use it for His good purposes. He used anti-Semitism to produce the great movement of Zionism, launched by Theodor Herzl, to re-birth the nation of Israel and bring millions of scattered Jews back into their homeland. This does not, however, obliterate the demonic source of all hatred of the Jewish people. After all, if the enemy can succeed in destroying the Jews altogether, he succeeds in proving God a liar, since He guarantees the survival of the nation of Israel.

> **"He who appoints the sun to shine by day, who decrees the moon and stars to shine by night, who stirs up the sea so that its waves roar – the Lord Almighty is his name: Only if these decrees vanish from my sight," declares the Lord, "will the descendants of Israel ever cease to be a nation before me."** (Jer. 31:35-6)

How else may we explain the survival of a remnant of Jews as a distinct people over the centuries, despite so many attempts to destroy them, when other ancient nations and civilizations have crumbled and disappeared? Also, if the enemy could destroy the Jews, he could succeed in preventing the return of the Messiah, the redeemer of Mankind, who would be born of Jewish descent (John 4:22). And, if the enemy succeeds in destroying Jerusalem, there would be no city for the Messiah to return to, since the word states his feet will stand on the Mount of Olives (Zech. 14).

CHAPTER FIVE

REPLACEMENT THEOLOGY

Balak, the king of Moab, out of hatred for Israel, sought in vain for Balaam to curse Israel three times, but Balaam could not curse those who the Lord had blessed. He proceeded to pronounce a blessing upon Israel instead. How has this anti-Semitic attitude slithered into the Christian Church? I know that many sincere Christians love Israel and the Jewish people, and this is not a rebuke towards them. I have had people come up to me in shock after a presentation on the history of Christian anti-Semitism, saying that they have never heard nor experienced any of this 'cursing' of the Jews in their Christian circle. The historical facts, however, testify for themselves, and we need to be aware of the history of our faith, including its dark side, in order that we may prevent future mistakes of the same nature with disastrous consequences. Most of this information is, unfortunately, not taught in Christian Bible Colleges. The truth is, however, that the Church became the instrument of hasatan (the adversary) to practice anti-Semitism on an ever-increasing scale as the Gentiles grew in numbers and divorced themselves from their Jewish roots.

Satan has succeeded in twisting the name of the Messiah into a Greek, gentile counterfeit in order that the name of salvation and incredible mercy would be perverted into one that evokes hatred and fear in the hearts of the ones He gave His life for. Millions of Jewish people were murdered in the very name of the One who came to save them. A Zionist Jew, Joseph Dunner, published the following statement: *"To Christians of all denominations – Jesus is the symbol of all that is pure, sacred and lovely. To Jews from the fourth century, Jesus became the symbol of anti-Semitism, of libel, of cruelty, of violent death."* [1] (Israel, October 1950).

This statement reveals in part why Jews, will not even entertain the notion that this 'Jesus' could be their Messiah – the one apparently responsible for the suffering and persecution that many of His followers have caused to the Jewish people. Indeed, I heard of a Jewish woman, sincerely seeking the Lord, who prayed this way, *"Oh God, please reveal the true Messiah to me. And dear God, please let him be anyone but Jesus."* Incredibly, Satan used those who call themselves followers of a Jewish Messiah to accomplish his evil purposes – stealing, killing, and destroying - against the Jewish people.

How could this possibly happen? Only through the very crafty plan of the enemy to appeal to the pride of the Church. That lying snake whispered into their ears that because the Jews, supposedly by their rejection of the Messiah (whereas their real sin was disobedience to the Torah and idolatry) were taken out of the land and scattered among the nations, that this was definite proof that God had abandoned them. Not understanding the everlasting nature of the covenant God made with Abraham and his descendants, the church began to believe that the Jews are no longer the 'chosen people of God' and that now THE CHURCH is the New Israel! The Church then 'spiritualised' all the scriptures regarding Israel and appropriated all the blessings, leaving all the curses upon the Jews. *"Of the 35,000 promises said to be made to Israel in the Old and New Testaments, over 30,000 are distinctly*

---

[1] Anton Darms, '*The Jew Returns to Israel*', pg. 113 (Zondervan Publishing House, Grand Rapids, Michigan, 1965).

given to Israel, and therefore, belong to Israel as a nation." [2]

This dangerous kind of thinking, that the Church has replaced Israel (rather than joined her) as 'God's chosen' still exists, believe it or not, in many of the mainstream churches today. In an Alliance church that had scheduled me to speak about the Passover, the pastor took me aside privately before the Sunday morning meeting to tell me that according to him, the Jews are no longer God's children; that the 'Church' is now the 'New Israel' – the chosen of God. He stood up in the pulpit and proceeded to teach this false doctrine to the congregation. But then he turned it over to me and the Lord gave me one hour with the two edged sword of the word of God to cut down all these lies. Halleluyah! This church invited me to return three more times to share from the word of God regarding Israel! Praise the Lord who uses the foolish and weak of this world to confound the wise.

I set up a book table and had opportunity to share for a few minutes on the Jewish Roots of Christianity at a woman's weekend retreat. God set the whole thing up for me, since the main speaker prepared the group by talking about our 'roots', showing us a beautiful slide show of flowers, ending with an exhortation about 'blooming where we're planted'. Really, it was lovely. She encouraged the women to look at their roots and re-connect with them in order to become more whole. What a lead off! Although she meant our families of origin, it was a perfect opportunity to encourage the women to examine the deeper roots of their Christian faith in a Jewish Messiah. Throughout the weekend, however, I became increasingly discouraged by the ignorance about the Jewish people and outright anti-Semitism displayed by several women, representing various different denominations of Christianity. It was almost as if, by my faith in Yeshua, they thought this gave them license to run down my own Jewish people – that now, I was somehow 'on the other side'. One woman came

---

2 *Ibid.* pg. 45

to me and lamented how *'difficult it is to get along with those Jews'*, and expected my complete agreement. I told her that my family is all Jewish and that although there are a few *'tough nuts'* in every family, I find them generally very agreeable people. *'Oh...',* she said. Thoughtful for a moment, she then piped up with what she thought was a gracious statement,

"Well, yes, I suppose we should give the Jews some respect, since they used to be God's chosen people."

"They still are", I answered. Pause.

"Yes...well..."

Sheepishly, she wandered off. Later, at the presentation (in which they gave me a maximum of ten minutes to share at 10:00 at night) this woman was front row center, nodding vigorously as the Holy Spirit convicted her of the Truth. Unfortunately many of the Church Fathers taught anti-Semitism from the pulpits.

Anti-Semitism in the Church
Quotes of the Church Fathers

Saint Gregory of Nyssa (335-394) stated of the Jews:

> "Slayers of the Lord, murderers of the prophets, adversaries of God, haters of God, men who show contempt for the law, foes of grace, enemies of their father's faith, advocates of the devil, brood of vipers, slanderers, scoffers, men whose minds are in darkness, leaven of the Pharisees, assembly of demons, wicked men, stoners, and haters of righteousness."

Saint John Chrysostom (334-407), who was called one of the greatest Christian orators of all times, (Golden-mouthed), a sweet and gentle soul, said this of the Jews: *"Of what to accuse*

the Jews?...inveterate murderers, destroyers, men possessed by the devil ...They know only one thing, to satisfy their gullets, get drunk, to kill and maim one another...they murder their offspring and immolate them to the devil...The synagogue is a place of shame and ridicule...the domicile of the devil, as is also the soul of the Jews...their rites are criminal and impure; their religion a disease...He who can never love Christ enough will never have done fighting against those Jews who hate Him...I hate the Jews..."
"The Jews are the most worthless of all men...They worship the devil, their religion is a sickness...The Jews are corrupt because of their odious assassination of Christ...no expiation possible, no indulgence, no pardon" [3]

Jews - Christ Killers?

This accusation of the Jew as 'Christ Killer' has been used to justify everything from beating up little Jewish boys walking home from Yeshiva (Jewish school of learning), to the mass genocide of six million men, women and children. Rick Aharon Chaimberlin, of Petah Tikvah (Door of Hope) ministry, tells the story in his article, 'Christ Killer', that even in the modern culture of 1967, in his college sociology class, a student from Italy stood up and protested the professors comment that violence wasn't nearly as great a problem in Jewish society as it was in Gentiles', saying, : *"But the Jews Killed Christ."* He adds, *"Back in the late 1970's,*

---

3 Source: Richard Booker, *'How the Cross Became a Sword'.*
Note: These, and other quotes of the church fathers are found in the following resources: *'The Guilt of Christianity Towards the Jewish People'*, Sister Pista, Evangelical Sisterhood of Mary. (For copies of this free information leaflet as well as suggestions for a service of repentence write to: Evangelical Sisterhood of Mary; Michael L. Brown, *'Our Hands are Stained with Blood: The Tragic Story of the "Church" and the Jewish People'*; Dr. William James Broadway, *'Has the Church Fallen Under a Curse?'*

we used to have a Hebrew-Christian come up to Rochester to speak with our fledgling Messianic fellowship. He related how he was called a "Christ-killer" by kids in the New York City neighborhood where he grew up during the Depression. They would attack him and force him to kiss a crucifix. Years later, he came to believe in Yeshua (who he called Jesus). A well-meaning lady gave him a crucifix to wear. Even though this gentleman had adopted much of Gentile Christian culture, he had a real problem with wearing the crucifix. He came up with a solution: He put the crucifix on the passenger seat of his car when he went shopping. He prayed that if God wanted him to have it, that it would still be there when he returned from the store. If God didn't want him to have it, he prayed that the crucifix would be gone. When he returned, he found that the crucifix had been stolen, much to his relief." [4]

In reality, the word of God tells us who was responsible for the actual death of Yeshua.

> **"We are going up to Jerusalem, and everything that is written by the prophets about the Son of Man will be fulfilled. He will be handed over to the Gentiles. They will mock him, insult him, spit on him, flog him and kill him. On the third day he will rise again."** (Luke 18:32-33)

Although some Jewish people were involved in the plot to kill him, the Sanhedrin (Jewish ruling council) did not have the power to carry out a sentence of capital punishment under Roman rule.

> **"'But we have no right to execute anyone,' the Jews objected."** (John 18:31)

---

4 Petah Tikvah (Door of Hope), 165 Doncaster Road, Rochester, NY 14623 USA Jan-March 2001 issue. Tevel-Adar 5761, VOL. 19, No. 1, pg. 3)

In fact, most of the Jewish people loved Yeshua so much that those planning to arrest him knew they could not do so during the Passover or they would have a riot on their hands.

> **"But not during the Feast," they said, "or there may be a riot among the people."** (Matt. 26:5)

Actually, the Jews desperately wanted to receive Yeshua as their conquering King to deliver Israel. Remember that all those shouting, *"Hosanna!"* and waving palm branches upon his arrival in Jerusalem riding on a colt, were not Christians celebrating 'Palm Sunday'; these were all Jews who honored and adored Yeshua (Mark 11:9). At times, Yeshua was forced to escape to a solitary place, knowing that the people would try to make him King, even by force.

After the people saw the miraculous sign that Yeshua did, they began to say,

> **"Surely this is the Prophet who is to come into the world. Yeshua, knowing that they intended to come and make him king by force, withdrew again to a mountain by himself."** (John 6:14-15)

The gospels all clearly show that many, many Jews put their trust and faith in Yeshua, therefore, to make a broad generalization that 'the Jews crucified Jesus' is absolutely ridiculous! If a political conspiracy formed amongst a small group of U.S. citizens to assassinate the president of the United States and they bribed and coerced some others to carry out the plot, would it be reasonable to condemn all Americans as 'President Killers'? What of the ones who actually carried out the execution? Is their entire race now labeled throughout historical time as 'President Killers'?

It is unbelievable how many Christians I meet don't even question this crucial point. They just assume what they have been told, that the Jews are 'Christ Killers'. I have found, though, that many Christians who believe this lie are not malicious, simply ignorant. At a Christian camp we attended one summer, I sat during a break, trying to prepare my notes. While on this exact issue of 'Who killed Christ?' the woman next to me struck up a conversation and asked what I was doing. Immersed in my task, I brushed her off at first with the answer that I was doing a personal Bible study. Undaunted, she questioned me further (the Holy Spirit can be quite persistent, I've noticed when the meeting is a divine appointment from Him). And so I shared a bit what I was working on. She immediately came up with the statement, *"But the Jews killed Christ, didn't they?"* We spent the next hour or so discussing this very important point.

Both Jews and Gentiles were responsible for Yeshua's death, but didn't he clearly state that this was in order that everything written by the prophets about him would be fulfilled? In fact, no one took his life from him. He laid it down of his own accord.

> **"I am the good shepherd; the good shepherd lays down His life for the sheep...no one has taken it away from Me, but I lay it down on My own initiative."** (John 10:11, 18)

Although no one took the life of our Savior against his will, we are all, every one of us, Jew and Gentile, responsible for his death, since he was slain as the Passover Lamb to atone for the sins of all mankind.

Why Can't Jews 'See' Jesus?

Christian anti-Semitism has built up a huge wall between the Jewish people and their own Messiah. The crimes perpetrated against the Jews by 'so-called' Christians have turned the name of Jesus Christ into a stumbling block and grave offense to the Jewish people. If these Christians would read the scriptures, however, they would see that it was in God's plan for the Jews to reject the Messiah. God himself, brought a temporary blindness upon their eyes. *Why?* In order that salvation could come to the Gentiles as well as the Jews.

> **"I do not want you to be ignorant of this mystery, brothers (and sisters), so that you may not be conceited: Israel has experience a hardening in part until the full number of the Gentiles has come in. And so all Israel will be saved, as it is written: The deliverer will come from Zion; he will turn godlessness away from Jacob. And this is my covenant with them when I take away their sins."** (Rom. 11:25-27)

That the deliverer is coming to save Israel is a given. God has planned it, purposed it, made every accommodation for it and it will happen!

> **"Yes, I have spoken, and I will bring it to pass; I have purposed it, and I will do it."** (Is. 46:11)

It is very important, however, that the Church not become arrogant in the meantime. Notice the hardening over Jewish hearts towards Yeshua is only in part and is only until a certain, pre-ordained time – when the fullness of the Gentiles has come in. God will choose when to soften the hearts of the Jewish people.

What is to be the attitude of the Church?

> **"If some of the branches have been broken off, and you, though a wild olive shoot, have been grafted in among the others and now share in the nourishing sap from the olive root, do not boast over those branches. If you do, consider this: You do not support the root, but the root supports you."** (Rom. 11:17-18)

What mercy and grace – the Lord temporarily set His chosen people aside in order to graft the Gentiles in among them. Where would these Gentile Christians be if the Jews had received the Messiah? They would still be strangers to the covenant, without God and without hope in this world (Eph. 2:12). Is this cause to despise the Jew, to drag old Jewish men into synagogues on Easter Sunday and pull out their beard? Is this cause to kick and beat and whip Jews on the street and throw their children into gas chambers? Is not a more appropriate response in the light of scripture for a Gentile Christian to find a Jew somewhere and give him a great, big hug, thanking him for making it possible that he might also be saved? (I wouldn't recommend this, by the way! There are other ways of expressing gratitude, making restitution, and repaying the debt owed to the Jewish people.)

Join me in grieving over other words spoken and written by church fathers:

St. John Chrystostom said, *"God hates the Jews and always hated the Jews...I hate the Jews also because they outrage the law."*

What is the truth in the Word of God?

> **"I have loved you, O My people, with an everlasting love and with loving kindness I have drawn you to Me."** (Jer. 31:3)

> "Because you are precious in My sight and honored and because I love you." (Is. 43:4)

> "For the Lord will not cast off His people, nor will He forsake His inheritance." (Ps. 94:14)

> "They are still His special ones." (Is. 14:1b)

The Crusades

During the Crusades, soldiers operating under a blanket of papal protection slaughtered thousands of Jews, screaming, *"The Jews have killed our Savior; they must convert or be killed."* Christian Crusaders marched around blazing synagogues singing Christian hymns, 'O Christ, we adore Thee', while the Jews locked inside burned to death along with their Torah scrolls, the Word of God, which became flesh and dwelt amongst us in the person of Yeshua Hamashiach (John 1:14).

My husband and I browsed through a Christian bookstore, trying to find any books on Messianic Judaism. These were in scarce supply, but what we did find, were Crusaders uniforms for children. Most people are completely unaware of the slaughter of Jewish people committed by these 'Christian Heroes'. When churches sing 'Onward Christian Soldier' do they realize that many of these soldiers murdered thousands of Jews?

Pope Innocent III (1160-1216 A.D.),

"The Jew who denies that Messiah has come, and that He is God, lies. Herod is the devil, the Jews demons."

The Fourth Lateran Council

In 1214 A.D. the Fourth Lateran Council met in Rome to determine the relationship between Christians and Jews. They decreed that all Jews wear a 'Jewish badge'. (Hitler used this policy to force the Jews to wear a yellow Star of David, to mark them for abuse and execution.) The Lateran Council also decreed that Jews could not hold public office. This was also used as an example by the Nazis to dismiss every Jew in Germany from civil service positions. In fact, over twenty anti- Jewish measures instituted to persecute and eventually exterminate the Jews by the Nazis were derived from Roman Catholic Canonical law.

The Spanish Inquisition (1491 A.D.)

Through torture and burning at the stake, hundreds of thousands of Jews were massacred throughout Spain in an attempt to force their 'conversion' to 'Christianity'. Human bonfires blazed day and night for three months burning Jews who would not 'convert' to Christianity. All this violence was done in the 'name of Christ' using the symbol of the cross. Is it any wonder that this cross, worn as jewelry by so many as a symbol of love, and saving grace is perceived as a symbol of butchery by the Jews? Paul says in Romans chapter 14 that if something we eat causes a brother or sister to stumble in their faith, then we are no longer acting in love. Might we not suggest the same with regards to what we wear on our person? If we go around wearing big crosses, or T-shirts of a bloody Christ on a cross, are we acting in love towards the Jewish people? When faced with the option of submitting to baptism or death, many Jews chose the path of martyrdom rather than bow to 'some foreign God'. "You shall have no other gods before Me" must have coursed through their minds as they faced death with the 'Shma' prayer on their lips:

שְׁמַע יִשְׂרָאֵל יְהוָה אֱלֹהֵינוּ יְהוָה אֶחָד

"Shma Yisrael Adonai Eloheinu, Adonai Echad."

Hear O Israel, the Lord (Yehovah) is Thy God the Lord is One." (Deut. 6:4)

The Russian Pogroms (1881-1921)

The Jews were persecuted with the formal approval of the Church. Jewish villages were razed, men beaten, and women raped. Anyone who has seen the production of 'Fiddler on the Roof' would probably remember the 'Papa', stuck with a lame horse just before the Sabbath, dialoguing with God. *"God, I know we are your chosen people…but couldn't you choose someone else for a change?"*

My own grandfather left his home and family at only twelve years old, never to see them again, because of the severity of the pogroms in Russia.

The Attitude of Martin Luther Towards the Jews

One of the greatest contributors to the cause of Christianity, who stood against the corruption of the Catholic Church and almost single-handedly translated the Bible into the German language was Martin Luther (1483-1546). Unfortunately, Luther revealed a lethal, venomous spirit towards the Jews. He said, *"Know this, Christian, you have no greater enemy than the Jew."* In his tract, "On the Jews and Their Lies", Martin Luther wrote that *"Jews should be enslaved because they were children of the devil and should never touch a Christian's hand. Luther demanded their synagogues be burned to the ground, their books destroyed, their homes laid waste, their cash and treasures be taken from them, their rabbis forbidden to teach and 'their tongues be cut out from their throats."* [5]

The following quote is taken from pages 49 and 50 of the 64 page booklet entitled, 'The Jews and Their Lies', by Dr. Martin Luther: *"Whenever you see or think about a Jew, say to yourself as follows: Behold the mouth which I see there has every Saturday cursed, execrated, and spit upon my dear Lord Jesus Christ, who has redeemed me with his precious blood; and also prayed and cursed before God that I, my wife and children, and all Christians should be stabbed, and perish in the most miserable manner – would like to do so himself if he could, that he might come into possession of our goods. Perhaps he has this very day often spit on the ground over the name of Jesu (according to their custom), and the spittle is still clinging to his mouth, and beard where there is still room for it. Should I eat with, drink with, or speak to such a devilish mug (mouth)? I might devour many devils as, for a certainty, I would become partakers of all the devils who live in that Jew, and would spit upon the precious blood of Christ. God keep me from doing that."* [6]

'Judensau'

A little known fact about Luther is that in the back of his church is the sculpture of a pig. It is called a Judensau (Jewish sow), erected to spite the Jews and commemorate their expulsion from the German town of Wittenberg in 1305. The Hebrew inscription, translated as 'Great is the name of the One who is blessed' is used

---

5 Erwin W. Lutzer, 'Hitler's Cross', (Moody Press, Chicago, 1995, pg. 86)

6 Michael Brown, '*Our Hands are Stained With Blood*', (Destiny Image Publisher, P.O. Box 310, Shippensburg, P.A., 17257, 1994).

in sarcasm to link the Jews and their God to the pig, a symbol of all which is unclean and unholy. This monument stands as a testament to the hatred of the German Christian Church towards the Jewish people. In 1988, a memorial was erected nearby to apologize that six million Jews died under the symbol of the cross. My question is, if their repentance runs true, why don't they completely destroy the whole disgusting piece of work?

Luther, although not excused, was following in the footsteps of his predecessors. Painful as it is to read these words, we must understand that this anti-Jewish attitude has passed down throughout the generations to this very day, even among many Christians. Many times, this is done subtly, not overtly, and the perpetrators would, I am certain, deny any anti-Semitism within their hearts. We watched, once, a dramatization of the life of Paul, performed by a church youth group. This group formed the nucleus of those who were teaching many children. It showed Paul trying in vain to convince several Jews that 'Jesus is the Lord', and then announcing in a tone of disgust and anger, *'These stubborn Jews will never listen, so I give up! I'm going to the Gentiles!"*

Is it any wonder that so many carry this kind of arrogant attitude towards the Jewish people?

I fear for the Christian anti-Semite especially, since for the heathen we may pray, 'Father, forgive them, for they don't know what they are doing'. For the Christian, however, there is no excuse, since God has given us His word to explain his wonderful plan of salvation for all of mankind, and how Israel and the Jewish people remain central to that plan. Many Christians cannot understand why these 'stubborn, stiff-necked people', the Jews, will not just accept Jesus and be saved. Is it any wonder, however, after understanding the tragic history between the Church and the Jewish people, why most Jewish people will not even consider a serious investigation that the one they call 'Jesus' may be the Messiah?

Missionary Go Home!

Once we comprehend the magnitude of the sin of the Church against the Jewish people, we can better understand the opposition of the Jew towards the gospel and Christian evangelistic efforts. 'Missionary' is one of the most hated words in Hebrew. The Jewish person reasons as follows: *"The Christians have tried to exterminate us for 2,000 years. Finally, we have found our way back to our own land with God's help, and what happens? The Christians follow right after us and tell us we should not be Jews anymore. We should convert to Christianity.... The Jew understands this (evangelizing) as an attempt to persuade God's chosen people into becoming a member of 'an idolatrous, heathen, idol-worshipping, Jew-persecuting religion."* [7]

The Christian Evangelism Under Attack

The right to evangelize in Israel is coming under attack in our day by proposed political bills in which it is proposed that all who preach their faith in public with the aim to persuade another of its correctness will be sentenced to imprisonment or large fines. This bill seemingly places all active Christian missionaries in danger of persecution and harassment for sharing their faith with the house of Israel. According to the Messianic Action Committee in Israel, this bill is the

> "trampling of freedom of expression and faith in Israel and the trampling of its democratic character."

---

[7] '*I Became as a Jew, What Jews and Christians Should Understand About Each Other*' by Shira Sorko-Ram of Maoz, Israel pgs. 9, 11, 12.

There are those who even hint that this bill mimics Nazi legislation and that those who support it have now turned from the persecuted into the persecutors.

Many non-religious Israelis, however, either don't care, or else readily accept legislation against Messianic Jews and Christians. One example is popular radio personality Tommy Lapid who gave an editorial on July 18th, 1998 on Israel's Station 2: *"The ad (against the bill) calls us to come out to defend democracy, and I refuse. I support Pinchasi's anti-democratic bill. From my perspective, all religion is superstition, but two thousand years of persecution have granted us the right to be left alone in our Land. If we hadn't been murdered, if we hadn't been forced to convert to Christianity, then today we would have been a nation of two hundred million people. The source of all anti-Semitism is Christianity; all the troubles that have come upon us are because of that rebel rabbi whom Christianity sees as the Messiah. Let them enjoy him, let them adore him, let them pray to him and let them believe that he is God, but not in our schools. Here we have immunity. We bought it with our blood."*

Indeed, the state of Israel arose out of the ashes and the blood of six million Jewish souls – men, women and children. Most Jewish people (and Christians as well) see the acceptance of 'Jesus' as a conversion to another religion called Christianity that is diametrically opposed to Judaism. We have a church on one side of the street, worshipping on Sundays, eating pork, abstaining from wine and dancing, and celebrating Christmas and Easter; while on the other side of the street, we have a Jewish synagogue (or Messianic congregation), worshipping on Shabbat (Saturday), eating kosher, blessing the wine and bread on Friday nights, dancing the Hora, and celebrating the Feasts of the Lord. How is this one faith in the same God? Therefore, most Jews see this Christian missionary activity as just another attempt to destroy the Jewish people, as deadly, if not more so, than the

Holocaust. The Jews have survived as a distinct people for over 4000 years of persecution, even though many other people groups have disappeared during this time. God has promised that they will never cease to be a nation of people before Him (Jer. 31:36). The threat of assimilation into Christian religion and culture is an ever-present danger to the Jewish people, and has never promised immunity or protection. The Jews in pre-war Germany considered themselves more German than Jewish. They thought that this assimilation into German, Christian culture would protect them from the growing Nazi movement. They were wrong.

Hitler Borrows Doctrine From the Church

Hitler's plot to exterminate the Jewish people in the Holocaust was not, as we can discern from the quotes of the Church Fathers, the independent plan of a demented madman; the Nazis used the doctrine of Church theologians as the foundation for their evil plan. Therefore, in the book outlining the plan for the 'final solution' to the Jewish problem, Mein Kampf, written while serving a prison sentence, Hitler stated, *"Hence today I believe that I am acting in accordance with the almighty Creator by defending myself against the Jews, I am fighting for the work of the Lord."* , *"The Holocaust did not begin with Hitler lining up the Jews outside the gas chambers. It began with religious leaders sowing the seeds of hatred toward Jews within their congregations."* [8]

The Holocaust did not happen in a theological vacuum but was a progression of a trend that originated with anti-Jewish 'Christian doctrine':

---

[8] John Hagee, *'Final Dawn over Jerusalem'*, (Thomas Nelson, Nashville, Tenn. 1998).

1. You have no right to live among us as Jews.
2. You have no right to live among us.
3. You have no right to live.

Love One Another

Anti-Semitism continues today because of ignorance of God's word and the resulting wrong beliefs. Replacement Theology is still preached from pulpits today. We must expose this vicious lie and cut it out of the Church with the two edged sword of the Word of God. Didn't the Lord tell us in his Word that His disciples would be known, not by their hatred, but by their love?

> **"A new command I give you: Love one another. As I have loved you, so you must love one another. By this all men will know that you are my disciples, if you love one another."** (John 13:34-35)

Paul said that no matter what he does, even for the Lord, whether speaking in the tongues of men and of angels, having the gift of prophecy and being able to fathom all mysteries and all knowledge; even if he has a faith that can move mountains, and gives all he possesses to the poor or even surrenders his body to the flames – still if he has not love, Paul says he is nothing (1 Cor. 13:1-3).

When asked which is the most important of all the commandments, the Lord could not answer with only one, since there were two of equal importance.

> **"Hear O Israel, the Lord our God, the Lord is one. Love the Lord your God with all your heart and with all your soul and with all your mind and with all your strength. The second is this: 'Love your neighbor as yourself. There is no commandment greater than these."** (Mark 12:29-31)

> **"Those who say they love God but hate anyone are like people stumbling around in the darkness, not knowing where they are going."** (1 John 2:10-11)

In fact, although they believe they are going to heaven, the Word of God says that anyone who hates another person is like a murderer, and that eternal life is not the inheritance of murderers, unless they repent and receive forgiveness (1 John 3:15). It is not my responsibility to judge my brother, as there is only one Judge. Nor am I to accuse, since the position as the accuser of the brethren has already been filled by hasatan, (the accuser in Hebrew). Thank goodness, I need not decide who is saved and who is not; I leave these matters that are too high for me to the Lord. We must, however, examine ourselves for any traces of this bitter poison of anti-Semitic doctrine. *"How odd of God to choose the Jew! But not as odd as those who choose the Jewish God, and hate the Jew!"* [9]

---

9 Edith Schaffer, '*Christianity is Jewish*'

CHAPTER SIX

RESPONSE OF THE NATIONS

Perhaps individuals may say, *"I am surely not anti-Semitic; no one in my family has ever spoken against the Jewish people, nor have I ever heard a word against them in my church."* The tendency may be to think, then, that one is 'off the hook' with God. Besides the collective guilt of the Church, however, we may investigate the record of the nations of the world with regards to their treatment of the Jewish people. Remember that the Word of God states that whoever curses Abraham's descendants through Jacob (Israel) is cursed. Let's examine the response of the nations to the plight of the Jews in pre-WW II Nazi Germany in this article by Peggy Mann.[1]

Prelude to Holocaust - Evian

In Evian-Les Bains, France, at the white splendor of the Royal Hotel in July 1938, the holocaust – the murder of two-thirds of Europe's Jews – could most likely have been halted. Here, in the famed French resort, 15 weeks after Hitler annexed Austria, delegates from 32 nations met to determine how they could

---

[1] At Evian in 1938, the world turned its back on European Jews. The Washington Post Outlook, Sunday, April 16, 1978.

rescue the Jews of the Greater German Reich and help them to re-establish their lives elsewhere. Never before in history had nations of the world gathered together for the single purpose of saving a doomed people. "Nations of Asylum", they called themselves. The conference, organized by President Franklin D. Roosevelt, appointed Myron C. Taylor as his special ambassador. Reporters from all 32 nations attended. One wrote, *"It is a test of civilization...Can America live with itself if it lets Germany get away with this policy of extermination, allows the fanaticism of one man to triumph over reason, refuses to take up this gage of battle against barbarism?"*

Who were these "Nations of Asylum"? Argentina, Australia, Brazil, Columbia, Denmark, the United States, Great Britain and her Commonwealth countries, France, Belgium, Sweden, Norway, the Netherlands, Switzerland, nations of Latin America and Africa. Only two countries, Italy and South Africa, turned down the invitation, but South Africa sent an observer. An uninvited contingent of observers also showed up: the Nazis. They took careful notes during all the proceedings. Also attending were top officials of 39 refugee organizations, including 20 Jewish agencies, who had come to present the delegates with eyewitness accounts, reports, and statistics, all of which culminated in one irrefutable conclusion: the Jews of Hitler's Reich were doomed unless they could get out of Germany and Austria.

And they could get out – at this time. The official German policy in 1938 was only to make the Reich 'Judenrein' (purified of Jews). They wanted to get the Jews out, but there was only one problem – who would let the Jews in? A sad 'joke' circulated among the Reich. A Jewish man goes to a travel agency, asking for the agent to make the necessary travel arrangements for him. The agent sets a globe on the counter and asks,

"Here is the world. Where do you want to go? Just choose."

The Jewish man spins the globe slowly and studies it carefully. After a long while, he finally looks up and says, *"Have you got anything else?"*

In fact, there was only one spot in the world where European Jewry would be welcomed: the land called Palestine. At least, they were welcomed by the Jews of Palestine, not the Arabs, and not the British who held the League of Nations Mandate to rule over Palestine. Dr. Chaim Weizman, President of the World Zionist Organization and the Jewish Agency, one of the most eloquent spokesman for promoting increased Jewish immigration to Palestine, was not allowed to speak. Also, a representative of the Yishuv, the Jewish delegation from Palestine, chosen for her direct forcefulness as a speaker, was also not allowed to speak. Her name was Golda Meyerson (Meir). All presentations from the 39 refugee organizations were scheduled for a single afternoon. Each representative was given only 10 minutes. As the afternoon wore on, the allocated time was cut to a mere five minutes. The World Jewish Congress, representing seven million Jews, received only five minutes to plead their cause. The delegation of the Jews of the Reich did not receive any time at all. They were told to 'submit a written memorandum' which would be included in the minutes.

Even during the limited time at their disposal, advocates for Jewish survival detailed horrors that had been happening for the past three months in Austria. Tens of thousands of Jews had been thrown into concentration camps…men, women, even small children were being cornered on the streets, beaten, kicked, and whipped by black-booted SS men…rabbis sent to clean the SS toilets…Jewish women forced down on their knees to scrub the gutters, often with acid added to the scrub water…throughout the country civilians were 'cooperating' with the SS by beating up Jews, evicting them from their flats, breaking into Jewish shops and homes, carting out anything of value. The explosion of terror and sadism even exceeded what had been seen in Germany.

In Austria, this had been happening for three months, since Hitler took over that country. In Germany, however, the systemic terrorism against the Jews began three years prior, starting officially with the Nuremberg Laws of September 15, 1935. Jews were no longer recognized as citizens; all Jews in the civil service had been fired. Jewish teachers and University professors were all fired. Jews were excluded from the entertainment industry, journalism, radio, the stock exchange, and law. By 1937, half the Jews in Germany were unemployed. Signs began appearing throughout the country on butcher shops, dairies, grocery stores, and pharmacies: 'NO JEWS ALLOWED'. In many towns, Jewish mothers could not buy milk for their children or medicine for those who became ill. Jewish children were required to attend segregated schools and even kindergartens bore the signs: 'Jewish Scum', or 'Cursed Be the Jew'. A brand new First Reader had been issued for small German Aryan children. In the section on religion, the youngsters read:

> "Remember that the Jews are children of the devil and murderers of mankind. Whoever is a murderer deserves to be killed himself."

A month prior to the Evian conference, the Great Synagogue of Munich was destroyed on Hitler's personal orders, followed by the destruction of synagogues in Nuremberg and Dortmund. In Buchenwald, Jews were whipped and tortured in the daytime. At night, a recorded voice continually shouted through a loudspeaker,

> "Any Jew who wishes to hang himself is asked first to put a piece of paper in his mouth with his number on it, so that we may know who he is."

Although most people believe that out of the six million annihilated Jews of the Holocaust, at least three to four million or more came from Germany and Austria. The truth is, however, that at the time of Evian, only 350,000 Jews resided in Germany and 220,000 in Austria. The 32 'Nations of Asylum', many of which had vast areas of unpopulated lands, could easily have agreed to save every Jewish man, woman and child in the German Reich! Let's see how many they actually did agree to save?

The United States

Taylor was the first to speak. All the other nations waited with great anticipation, as it was the U.S. that had organized the conference *"To uphold those principles that we have come to regard as the standards of our civilization."*

Some delegates wondered whether the United States would agree to accept all of the Reich's 570,000 Jewish refugees. Note: A generation later, the United States accepted 580,000 Cuban and Vietnamese refugees, with no noticeable ill effects on the economic life of the nation. Carefully, Ambassador Taylor explained that the United States had its quota system that could not be changed. The total German quota was set at 25,957 per year, however the U.S. agreed to lift the severe restrictions so that the full quota of 27,730 German and Austrian immigrants would be admitted each year.

There was a stunned silence as the ambassador sat down. This was the great gesture of hope and help offered by the nation populated by immigrants, the nation that for generations had offered asylum to Europe's oppressed?

The Other Nations

Thirty-one other nations were yet to be heard from. Surely they would find room for the refugees: Canada, the second largest nations in the world; Brazil, the fifth largest; Australia, the sixth largest. Between them they could easily absorb all the half-million would-be refugees. The Canadian delegate explained that Canada could accept only experienced agricultural workers. Columbia, Uruguay and Venezuela had the same immigration restrictions. What about Brazil? Just before coming to the conference, Brazil had enacted a brand new law – every visa application must be accompanied by a certificate of baptism. So unfortunately, Brazil could not accept any Jews at all! Australia? The entire continent had a population of the city of London. In fact, 'Populate or perish' was a popular Australian slogan. And yet, the Australian delegate, Lt. Col. J.W. White, explained that Australia could accept only 15,000 Jewish immigrants over a three-year period. *"As we have no real racial problem, we are not desirous of importing one."*

(In actuality, from 1933 to 1943, only 9,000 entered the country.) The British delegate had similar concerns. A rush of Jewish refugees from the Reich *"might arouse anti-Semitic feeling in Great Britain."* Nor did the British colonial empire contain territory suitable for the large-scale re-settlement of the refugees. No mention was made of Palestine. The French delegate announced that his country had already "reached the saturation point." Nicaragua, Costa Rica, Honduras, all classified intellectuals and merchants as 'undesirables.' Unfortunately, half the Jews in Germany and Austria fell into the 'intellectual' category: doctors, lawyers, professors; most of the rest were businessmen (merchants). The Swiss delegate complained about the 'inundation' of Jewish refugees after the fall of Austria to Hitler. Three or four thousand had already fled across the border, and unless the flow stopped, he warned that, *"Switzerland, which has as little use for these Jews as has Germany, will herself take measures to protect Switzerland from being swamped by Jews with the connivance of the Viennese police."*

And on and on it went. One delegate after another rose with a similar message: yes, the situation for Jews in the Reich is, indeed, horrendous. Unfortunately, however, his country's laws prevent any concrete aid. But each nation was certain that the other nations would open their doors. Only three small countries expressed willingness to help. Holland, the most densely populated of the Evian nations, with 800 people per square mile, had already taken in more than 25,000 Jewish refugees, but offered itself as a country of temporary asylum. The Germans invaded two years later, and by the end of the war, 75% of the Jews in Holland had perished. The Danish delegate stated that his overcrowded country would continue to accept refugees. Denmark took in and protected 1,500 Jews. The Dominican Republic announced that it would settle 100,000 refugees, however, only 500 found a home there.

Even these few positive proposals were drowned out by the official resolution passed unanimously on the final day of the Evian conference. *"The delegates of the Countries of Asylum are not willing to undertake any obligations toward financing involuntary immigration."*

In simpler words, only those Jews who could afford to pay their own way would be accepted. Since it had been clearly brought out at the conference that no Jew was permitted to leave Germany or Austria with more than 10 Reichsmarks (less than $5), that simple resolution made every Jew from Germany and Austria officially and automatically unacceptable to the "Countries of Asylum."

At the request of some of the South American delegates, 'contentious allusions' to the Third Reich were omitted in the final resolution. The delegates appointed a committee to study the matter further, under the direction of George Rublee, an American lawyer. Committee headquarters were set up in London.

Kristallnacht

On November 9th and 10th, only four months after Evian, came Kristallnacht (Crystal Night), so named after the glass that littered the streets from the windows of Jewish homes and businesses, the ghastly government-sponsored campaign of arson, mayhem and terror aimed exclusively at the Jews of Germany and Austria. It was the worst pogrom the modern world had, as yet, known, and outrage replaced apathy as tens of thousands of citizens of the Countries of Asylum petitioned their governments to immediately open their doors to the imperiled Jews of the Reich. George Rublee put forth a simple plan. Each of the 32 nations should immediately accept 25,000 Jews each. If only half of the 32 nations had agreed, every Jew in the Reich could have been saved.

None agreed.

During the four months since the Evian Conference, some of the nations of asylum, including Argentina, Mexico, Chile and Uruguay, rather than open their doors, had adopted new and even more restrictive immigration regulations, specifically designed to keep the Jews out. What about the U.S.? President Roosevelt held a press conference on November 15th, which included the statement: *"The news of the past few days from Germany has deeply shocked public opinion in the United States...I myself could scarcely believe that such things could occur in a 20th century civilization."*

When asked if the president would recommend a temporary change in the 'immigration laws so that more refugees would be allowed to enter the United States, he replied that no such changes were being considered. Was the U.S. contemplating breaking trade relations with the Third Reich?

"No", said the president.

Most of the rest of the nations of asylum expressed their strong disapproval of Kristallnacht, but none modified their immigration laws in order that the Reich's Jews could be saved.

Golda Meir later wrote, *"After the conference at Evians-les-Baines, it became chillingly clear that the Jewish people were entirely 'on their own'."*

German Reaction to Evian

The Evian conference took place eight months before Germany's annexation of Czechoslovakia, 14 months prior to the Nazi invasion of Poland and the outbreak of World War II. Could the holocaust have been halted at Evian? Of course no one can second-guess history, but if world opinion had been backed by world action, it seems almost inconceivable that Hitler would have proceeded with his 'final solution to the Jewish problem.' What is certainly clear is that, in Hitler's view, the Evian conference gave him carte blanche to go ahead. Just prior to the conference, Hitler had said in a speech at Konigsberg, *"I can only hope and expect that the other world, which has such deep sympathy for these criminals, will at least be generous enough to convert this sympathy into practical aid. We, on our part, are ready to put all these criminals at the disposal of these countries, for all I care, even on luxury ships."*

In a speech made immediately after the conference, Hitler

derided *"The other world is oozing sympathy for the poor, tormented people, but remains hard and obdurate when it comes to helping them."*

The reaction in Nazi newspapers may be summed up in a single sentence: *"The Evian Conference serves to justify Germany's policy against Jewry."*

On November 22nd, 1938, four months after Evian, a front page article appeared in Das Schwarze Korps, official newspaper of the Gestapo: *"Because it is necessary, because we no longer hear the world's screeching and because, after all, no power on earth can hinder us, we will now bring the Jewish question to its totalitarian solution."*

Note: The author of this article visited Evian in 1978 and found one man who remembered: Rene Richler, the elderly concierge at the Royal Hotel, who was a concierge at the time of the conference. Asked what he remembered about the conference, he told the author, *"Oh, yes, I remember the Evian Conference well. Very important people were here and all the delegates had a nice time. They took pleasure cruises on the lake. They gambled at night in the casino. They took mineral baths and massages... some of them took the excursion to go summer skiing. Some went riding... Some played golf. Meetings? Yes, some attended the meetings. But, of course, it is difficult to sit indoors hearing speeches when all the pleasure that Evian offers are waiting right outside."*

One particularly tragic incident concerns the voyage of the "St. Louis" (May-June 1939). On May 13th, the liner left Germany with 930 Jewish refugees. 734 held U.S. quota numbers, permitting entry to the U.S.A. All held Cuban landing certificates, although the Cuban authorities began raising doubts about the validity of these documents. On May 27th, the St. Louis docked at Havana. Only 22 refugees were allowed to land. On June 2nd, the Cuban Government ordered the St. Louis to leave Cuban territorial waters. June 3rd – U.S. State Department rejected the proposal that the refugees with U.S. quota numbers be allowed to land in the U.S.A. The St. Louis sailed along the Florida coast. American Jews offered the Cubans financial guarantees amounting to a million dollars for allowing the refugees to land at the Cuban port. The Cuban government permitted the refugees to camp on the Isle of Pines but a day later withdrew the offer. On June 6th, President Roosevelt received a telegram begging the U.S. to reconsider its refusal to provide a shelter for the refugees. He did not reply. Captain Gustav Shroeder feared a "collective suicide pact" among his 917 German Jewish refugee passengers, who were scheduled to sail back to Hamburg the next day. Hundreds of the refugees were threatening to take their lives if the ship sailed back to Germany. *"The disappointment was great. We could not understand how America, this giant country, would not permit us to enter – anywhere. Yes, to our great sorrow, that was the situation - all of huge America was locked!"* (Herta Fink-Hortig, St. Louis Passenger, Eyewitness account)

June 6th-9th – The St. Louis returned to Europe. Chile, Paraguay, Argentina and Columbia all refused any passenger asylum. The Captain contemplated 'beaching' the ship on the English coast to prevent its return to Germany.

Finally, Britain, Holland, Belgium, and France agreed to take some of the refugees. On June 17th, the refugees landed at Antwerp. The 819 sheltered in Europe came under German rule within 12 months and in 1944, were sent to Treblinka and other Nazi death camps. The 287 refugees accepted by Britain were interned behind barbed wire as 'enemy aliens', but survived.

The following quote from the book *'None is too Many'*, co-authored by Irving Abella and Harold Troper, reflects the heart of a nation whose ethnically selective immigration policies held back God's chosen ones. Frederick Blair, "a religious man, an elder in his church, a dedicated civil servant," was appointed director of Immigration in 1935. He set the policies and nothing that touched his department escaped his scrutiny. And from the point of view of European Jewry this was most unfortunate. Just when they most needed a friend at the gate, they had an enemy; instead of the philo-Semite they required, they had an anti-Semite. *"During the war years, the world seemed to be divided into two parts - those places where the Jews could not live, and those where they could not enter. Canada was in the latter camp."*

Note: As an update, here is a report from 'Watchmen' on the Ottawa Repentance meeting, November 5th, 2000. The 'FRIENDS OF THE ST. LOUIS REPORT'

"Seeking a safe haven from the terrors of the Nazi regime, the St. Louis was turned away from our nation sixty-one years ago. Representatives from the church in Canada invited the remaining survivors to Canada to officially welcome them and ask their forgiveness for the church's silence at a time when they so desperately needed our friendship. Repentance and reconciliation were on the hearts of church leaders, as some two hundred fifty came from many parts of the nation representing several denominations, cultures and generations. Israel holds the key to every nation seeking to fulfill its destiny in God! It has been revealed in recent years to the church in Canada that our history is darkened with acts of anti-Semitism. We felt led of the Lord as representatives of the Canadian church to take corporate responsibility for the atrocities of the past. There was a time when Canada closed her ears to the cries of distress of God's Chosen People, the apple of His eye. For this we are

most repentant. The journey began when God revealed to David Demian, director of Watchmen for the Nations, that the root sin of anti-Semitism must be dealt with in order for this nation to fulfill her destiny in God. David believes "If Canada repents, we're going to see God's power released for much healing in our land."

In light of this revelation about Canada's root sin, the church, culminating with the July 1, 1999 national repentance in Winnipeg, Manitoba, undertook many initiatives. We believe God accepted our repentance and our contrite hearts. The church in Canada rose up *for such a time as* this to own the mistakes of the past and identify with the sins of our forefathers. (May the believers in other nations follow their lead.

"For if they remain silent..." (Esth. 4:14-15)

CHAPTER SEVEN

REMEMBER AMALEK!

God has a long memory when it comes to attacks against his people Israel. He remembered the attack of Amalek and generations later, executed divine punishment.

> **"Remember what the Amalekites did to you along the way when you came out of Egypt. When you were weary and worn out, they met you on your journey and cut off all who were lagging behind; they had no fear of God...you shall blot out the memory of Amalek from under heaven. Do not forget!"** (Deut. 25:17-19)

Only those with no fear of God would dare attack the Jewish people, the apple of God's eye. This is a dire warning towards both individuals and nations that have mistreated the Jewish people over the centuries. The time will surely come for the day of reckoning. Any astute student of the Bible, however, knows that under the Mosaic covenant, God cursed the Jews for their sin and disobedience. God warned His people again and again, just as parents will warn their children of the consequences of their disobedience, but the wayward children would not listen to their Father.

> "I warned them again and again, saying, 'Obey me'. But they did not listen or pay attention; instead they followed the stubbornness of their evil hearts. So I brought on them all the curses of the covenant I had commanded them to follow but that they did not keep." (Jer. 11:7-8)

Curses of the Mosaic Covenant

What were the curses of the covenant? These are outlined in Deuteronomy chapter 28:

> "All these blessings will come upon you and accompany you if you obey the Lord your God... However, if you do not obey the Lord your God and do not carefully follow all his commands and decrees I am giving you today, all these curses will come upon you and overtake you...You who were as numerous as the stars in the sky will be left but few in number, because you did not obey the Lord your God..." (Deut. 28: 2,15,62)

What was the most severe punishment inflicted by God on His children? It was their global exile – the loss of their right to live at home in the land God gave to them.

> "Then the Lord will scatter you among all nations, from one end of the earth to the other...There the Lord will give you an anxious mind, eyes weary with longing, and a despairing heart. You will live in constant suspense, filled with dread both night and day, never sure of your life." (Deut. 28:64-66)

As any parent can attest who has been forced into the position of barring a rebellious teen from the family home, the pain felt is immense and the decision not taken lightly. It is a last-ditch move of desperation – of tough love – of saying 'I must draw the line here and cannot stretch it back any further.' The grown child must either conform into some measure of obedience or else leave home.

If it is God, Himself, who cursed the Jewish people, would it not be a legitimate question to ask if all those who persecuted them in the lands of exile were not, as Hitler said, simply carrying out the divine will of the Almighty? Hitler stated that in destroying the Jews, he believed himself to be carrying out the divine will of the Almighty God. Signs above the concentration camp barracks read, 'We do this to you in the name of Jesus Christ'. Many who participated in the persecution of the Jews in their lands of exile, or those who ignored their cries for help, considered it their religious duty – that they were only aiding and abetting a vengeful God who cursed the Jews for rejecting Christ.

We can look at this in several ways, but it needs to be dealt with because so many Christians mistakenly believe the Jews to be under God's curse until they 'believe in Jesus'. First of all, God did not curse the Jewish people for 'rejecting Jesus'. Nowhere in scripture does it indicate this as His motive. We discussed earlier how the blindness of the Jewish people towards their Messiah was part of God's overall plan and is only temporary (until the time of the Gentiles is fulfilled). The Jews were cursed for their disobedience to Torah, God's commandments.

If we look at another of God's curses, we may see a different perspective. When Eve disobeyed God in the Garden of Eden, He pronounced a curse upon her that has continued throughout the generations even until today.

> "To the woman he said, 'I will greatly increase your pains in childbearing; with pain you will give birth to children.'" (Gen. 3:16)

Would we be righteous, then, in deliberately and maliciously increasing the pain of women in bearing children simply because God pronounced this as a curse upon women? Of course not, in fact we do whatever we can, out of mercy, to alleviate this pain. This should have been the response of the Gentiles, especially Christians, to the suffering of the Jewish people.

> "Blessed are the merciful, for they shall be shown mercy." (Matt. 5:7)

Also, we may look at God's own view that is profoundly different than these merciless persecutors:

> "I am very jealous for Jerusalem and Zion, but I am very angry with the nations that feel secure. I was only a little angry, but they helped with evil intent....for whoever touches you touches the apple of his eye." (Zech. 1:14-15; 2:8)

There exists an enormous difference between a father administering discipline and a cruel bully, beating another man's child to death. Yes, God's judgment was severe upon His people, but He deals with His children in perfect justice.

> "The Lord is merciful and gracious, slow to anger, and abounding in mercy. He will not always strive with us, nor will He keep His anger forever. He has not dealt with us according to our sins, nor punished us according to our iniquities. For as the heavens are high above the earth, so great is His mercy towards those who fear Him; As far as

> the east is from the west, so far has He removed our transgressions from us. As a father pities his children, so the Lord pities those who fear Him. For he knows our frame; He remembers that we are dust." (Ps. 103:8-14)

Yes, our God is merciful and slow to anger; he loves and pities His children; but He has His limits. He is not a kindly, old, indulgent grandfather who allows his grandchildren to get away with anything since he knows he can send them back to their parents for discipline. He is a God of love and mercy, by also the God of justice and vengeance. We do others and ourselves no service but holding onto and passing on a one-sided view of the Almighty. He is to be loved, but He is also to be feared! Notice that in this same Psalm, God's mercy is conditional:

> "But the mercy of the Lord is from everlasting to everlasting on those who fear Him, and His righteousness to children's children, to such as keep His covenant, and to those who remember His commandments to do them." (Ps. 103:17-18)

A Day of Vengeance - To Uphold Zion's Cause

> "Come near, you nations and listen; pay attention you peoples!...The Lord is angry with all nations; his wrath is upon all their armies...For the Lord has a day of vengeance, a year of retribution, to uphold Zion's cause." (Is. 34:1, 2, 8)

God does not simply forget sin; individuals and nations cannot sweep their anti-Semitic attitudes and actions under some sort of cosmic carpet. We usually think of the Lord as a gentle man in a long, white robe, surrounded by children. But this was the meek Lamb of God who died for our sins. With His return to earth, He is coming as a mighty man of war to judge the earth, slay the wicked, and to execute vengeance – for Zion's sake.

Isaiah speaks of the 'Servant of the Lord' upon whom God will put His Spirit. This individual will bring justice to the nations and establish justice on earth. He will be

> **"A covenant for the people and a light for the Gentiles, to open eyes that are blind, to free captives from prison, and to release from the dungeon those who sit in darkness."** (Is. 42:1, 4, 6-7)

This is the prophesied redeemer who will not only bring Jacob back to God and gather Israel, but will also be a **"light for the Gentiles"** and bring God's salvation to the ends of the earth (Is. 49:6). Indeed, this is Yeshua the Messiah, whose very name means salvation.

> **"On the Shabbat (the Sabbath day), he went into the synagogue, as was his custom. And he stood up to read. The scroll of the prophet Isaiah was handed to him. Unrolling it, he found the place where it is written: 'The Spirit of the Sovereign Lord is upon me, because the Lord has anointed me to preach good news to the poor. He has sent me to proclaim freedom for the prisoners and recovery of sight for the blind, to release the oppressed, to proclaim the year of the Lord's favor.' Then he rolled up the scroll, gave it back to the attendant and sat down. The eyes of everyone in the synagogue were fastened on him, and he began by saying to them, 'Today this scripture is fulfilled in your hearing.'"** (Luke 4:16-21)

If we look at this scripture in Isaiah that Yeshua read, found in our Bibles in chapter 61, we can see that the prophecy continues with the words, **"...and the day of vengeance of our God."** (Is. 61:2b), followed by beautiful promises about the restoration of Israel through a future everlasting covenant. Why did Yeshua not read this portion? Because the continuation of this prophecy regarding the day of vengeance of God on the nations and the spiritual restoration of Israel belongs to His second coming! This day is coming:

> **"For the Lord has a day of vengeance, a year of retribution, to uphold Zion's cause."** (Is. 34:8)

Where were the Christians in these 'Nations of Asylum'? I know of an Egyptian Pastor who is leading the call within Christian Canada to national repentance; for the part this nation has played in closing their ears to the pleading of the Jews of Europe for help. Prime Minister Mackenzie King callously declared, *"One Jew in Canada is too many!"* [1]

On April 13th, 1999, a trainload of intercessors left Vancouver for Winnipeg to intercede for the nation of Canada – to ask forgiveness for Canada's history of anti-Semitism. On July 1st, Canada Day in Winnipeg, the National Day of Repentance has been set. All eight survivors of the St. Louis boat were invited to receive this Canadian token of Christian repentance for turning the ship away from Canadian borders. Each person attending brought a memorial stone to build an altar of repentance in Winnipeg. May the Lord honor their heartfelt prayers, for He has promised,

---

[1] Abella Irving and Harold Troper, '*None Is Too Many: Canada and the Jews of Europe*', 1933-1948, (published 1983 by Lester Publishing Limited, 56 The Esplanade, Toronto, Ontario M5E 1A7).

> "If my people, who are called by my name, will humble themselves and pray and seek my face and turn from their wicked ways, then will I hear from heaven and will forgive their sin and will heal their land." (2 Chron. 7:14)

May God raise up Christian leaders from every nation to call their people to repent for their country's sins against the Jewish people. God is now crying out to Gentile Christians – those adopted into the family of God:

> "'Where is your brother?' The Lord says, 'What have you done? Listen! Your brother's blood cries out to me from the ground.'" (Gen. 4:10)

Some Christians on pilgrimages across Europe, are retracing the steps of the Crusaders, washing away the spilled blood of the Jews with their tears of repentance. This is our only hope. If believers will not lead the way, then who will stand in the gap for their nation? Will the ungodly and non-believer – those with no knowledge of the Word of God- make crucial decisions in righteousness?

John Chretien, when he was Prime Minister of Canada, in an apparent hardening of Canada's position, told Palestinian leader Yasser Arafat that Israel could not delay forever before agreeing to a Palestinian state. *"We believe that through the negotiations we should resolve the creation of the state for the Palestinians,"* Chretien told a joint news conference with Arafat after two and a half hours of talks.[2]

Former American President, Bill Clinton, continually applied more and more pressure upon Israel to divide up this land. God declares that the land belongs to Him and is not to be sold or given

---

2 CNN interactive March 24, 1999.

away on any terms.

> "The land must not be sold permanently, because the land is mine and you are but aliens and my tenants." (Lev. 25:23)

This is what God says in response to those pressuring Israel to divide up this tiny land even further:

> "I will gather all nations and bring them down to the Valley of Jehoshaphat (Judgment). There I will enter into judgment against them concerning My inheritance, My people Israel, for they scattered My people among the nations and divided up My land." (Joel 3:2)

In the year 2006, to the horror of most God-fearing Israelis, Ariel Sharon, acting Prime Minister of Israel, gave away areas of Israel to the Palestinians, uprooting Jewish settlers from their land. Shortly afterwards, Sharon suffered a massive stroke.

Judgement of the Nations

Some believe, such as David Wilkerson, that the nations, including America, have already crossed the line beyond which God will no longer hear petitions for mercy. His judgment has been sealed. It is too late. The ever-increasingly disturbing weather patterns and natural disasters is evidence of this. In 1999 a hurricane four times the size of the one that leveled Ft. Lauderdale, Florida, in the past rage off the coast of the U.S.A. Some prophets today are predicting revival and continued prosperity for God's people, but God's true prophets know that God's judgment on the nations is already on its way. He has warned, but people have not listened. God is not mocked.

He is preparing to rise up in judgment upon the nations. Major earthquakes have devastated Greece, Turkey, and now Taiwan, killing thousands. In the year 2004, on Christmas Day, a tsunami devastated Indonesia, killing over a hundred thousand people. Floods totally destroyed New Orleans in 2005, a week before the planned homosexual gathering called South Decadence. Most Christian leaders who warn of this coming judgment point out the rampant sin, immorality and wickedness as the cause of God's wrath, but few understand the role that Israel and the Jewish people play in this whole end-times scenario.

David Demien, ironically an Egyptian pastor, made the following bold statement:

> *"The fate of Canada and the nations depends on the way they now deal with 'the Jewish issue."* [3]

The Word of God speaks of judgment on the nations:

> **"This is what the Sovereign Lord says: I speak in my jealous wrath because you have suffered the scorn of the nations. Therefore this is what the Sovereign Lord says: I swear with uplifted hand that the nations around you will also suffer scorn."** (Ezek. 36:6-7)

> **"The day of the Lord is near for all nations. As you have done, it will be done to you; your deeds will return upon your own head."** (Obad. 1:15)

---

3 *'Operation Esther'* meeting in Edmonton-Alberta, Canada in 1998.

I am not certain if, as Pastor Wilkerson states, the nations have committed such abominable sins that God will no longer forgive; if the nations have 'sinned away their day of grace'. I don't know if it's too late to turn back or avert the hand of God's judgment. It seems to me that He has already shown an incredible patience, giving every opportunity for the people to repent. His word contains several scriptures outlining His planned destruction of the nations of the Earth, and His mercy towards Israel.

Justice and Mercy

> "Do not fear, O Jacob my servant; do not be dismayed, O Israel. I will surely save you out of a distant place, your descendants from the land of their exile. Jacob will again have peace and security and no one will make him afraid. Do not fear, O Jacob my servant, for I am with you," declares the Lord. "Though I completely destroy all the nations among which I scatter you, I will not completely destroy you." (Jer. 46:27-28)

> "O people of Zion, who live in Jerusalem, you will weep no more. How gracious he will be when you cry for help! As soon as he hears, he will answer you...See, the Name of the Lord comes from afar, with burning anger and dense clouds of smoke; his lips are full of wrath, and his tongue is a consuming fire...He shakes the nations in the sieve of destruction...The Lord will cause men to hear his majestic voice and will make them see his arm (Yeshua) coming down with raging anger and consuming fire, with cloudburst, thunderstorm and hail." (Is. 30:19, 27-30)

> "So the Lord Almighty will come down to do battle on Mount Zion and on its heights. Like birds hovering overhead, the Lord Almighty will shield Jerusalem; He will shield it and deliver it, He will 'pass over' it and will rescue it." (Is. 31:4-5)

This will be the greatest 'Pass-over' Israel has every experienced! But just as in ancient Egypt, the Lord will once again make a distinction between those who are 'His people' and those who are not in special covenant relationship with Him. Those who make the mistake of ignoring the Word of the Lord and remain outside the protective blood covering of covenant will surely be destroyed.

> "'The terror you inspire and the pride of your heart have deceived you...Though you build your nest as high as the eagles' from there I will bring you down,' declares the Lord. 'Edom will become an object of horror; all who pass by will be appalled and will scoff because of all its wounds. As Sodom and Gomorrah were overthrown, along with their neighboring towns.'" (Jer. 49:16-18)

And what of Israel?

> "But I will bring Israel back to his own pasture"...In those days, at that time, declares the Lord, "search will be made for Israel's guilt, but there will be none, and for the sins of Judah, but none will be found, for I will forgive the remnant I spare...The Lord has opened his arsenal and brought out the weapons of his wrath, for the Sovereign Lord Almighty has work to do in the land of the Babylonians...how the

> Lord our God has taken vengeance, vengeance for
> his temple." (Jer. 50:19-20, 25, 28)

The Abrahamic Covenant

As these scriptures and others indicate, judgment is coming upon all the nations, but mercy upon Israel. How can this be? It is certainly not on the basis of the righteousness of the people of Israel today! Anyone who visits this land for even a short period of time can probably attest to that. I sometimes feel sorry for any Christian who makes a pilgrimage to Israel, expecting to find the Jews a 'Holy People'. One day, they will be, but that day has not yet come. Recently, I witnessed a physical brawl break out between several Ethiopian and Eastern European Jewish women in a local neighborhood. The hair pulling and shrieking was a terrible sight to see. The cynical side of me inside thought, "Ah yes, just another day in the 'Holy Land'." But God has great and wonderful promises to fulfill in this land and in this people. Although Israel was cursed and severely judged under the conditional nature of the Mosaic Covenant due to their conduct, God's covenant with Abraham is unconditional and forever. It still stands today.

> **"I will make you into a great nation and I will bless you; I will make your name great, and you will be a blessing. I will bless those who bless you, and whoever curses you I will curse; and all peoples on earth will be blessed through you...To your offspring I will give this land."** (Gen. 12:2-3, 7)

God, true to the faithfulness of His nature, must honor this oath to Abraham or else put His reputation in jeopardy. After all, if God could so easily break covenant with Abraham - that he swore by oath and sealed with blood - what is our assurance that

God will not also break His covenant with us as 'New Covenant believers'?

Not For Your Sake

Notice that when God speaks of restoring the Jewish people to the land and blessing them once again, it is because His very name is profaned when His people wander in exile, homeless, and at the mercy of the Gentiles. It casts a slur upon God's nature as a covenant keeping God.

> **"It is not for your sake, O house of Israel, that I am going to do these things, but for the sake of my holy name, which you have profaned among the nations where you have gone. I will show the holiness of my great name, which has been profaned among the nations, the name you have profaned among them. Then the nations will know that I am the Lord, declares the Sovereign Lord, when I show myself holy through you before their eyes."** (Ezek. 36; 22-23)

What are all these wonderful things that God has promised to do for Israel – for His own name's sake ?

> **"For I will take you out of the nations; I will gather you from all the countries and bring you back into your own land. I will sprinkle clean water on you, and you will be clean; I will cleanse you from all your impurities and from all your idols. I will give you a new heart and put a new spirit in you; I will remove from you your heart of stone and give you a heart of flesh. And I will put my Spirit in you and**

move you to follow my decrees and be careful to keep my laws. You will live in the land I gave your forefathers; You will be my people, and I will be your God...I want you to know that I am not doing this for your sake, declares the Sovereign Lord. Be ashamed and disgraced for your conduct, O house of Israel!" (Ezek. 36:24-28,32)

"I will surely gather them from all the lands where I banish them in my furious anger and great wrath; I will bring them back to this place and let them live in safety. They will be my people, and I will be their God. I will give them singleness of heart and action, so that they will always fear me for their own good and the good of their children after them. I will make an everlasting covenant with them: I will never stop doing good to them, and I will inspire them to fear me, so that they will never turn away from me. I will rejoice in doing them good and will assuredly plant them in this land with all my heart and soul...so will I give them all the prosperity I have promised them...because I will restore their fortunes, declares the Lord...Nevertheless, I will bring health and healing to it; I will heal my people and will let them enjoy abundant peace and security...I will cleanse them from all the sin they have committed against me and will forgive all their sins of rebellion against me. Then this city will bring me renown, joy, praise and honor before all nations on earth that hear of all the good things I do for it; and they will be in awe and will tremble at the abundant prosperity and peace I provide for it." (Jer. 32:37-42; 33:6-9)

CHAPTER EIGHT

THE SET TIME FOR MERCY ON ZION

Psalm 102:13 says,

> "You will arise and have mercy on Zion; for the time to favor her, Yes, the set time has come."

How can we know when this time is to occur? When, exactly, is this 'set time', and has it come at this time? The prophetic scriptures and current events combine to give us the answer to this question.

End of the Punishment

The punishment of the Jewish people under the Mosaic Covenant was temporary; it had a definite beginning and ending. It is crucial that we deal with this issue, in order that we may have an answer for those who believe that the Jews are still under a curse from God – the 'curse of the Law'. Just as when we discipline a child with a 'time out' or period of 'grounding', there is always (or should always be) an end to the punishment. Just as it would not be fair of us, as parents, to tell a younger child to go to his or her room forever, or that a teenager is grounded for the rest of his life (and into eternity), so it is not the way of a righteous God to treat His people with such injustice. How long was the punishment to last? The word of God gives us several signs.

Seven Times

In Leviticus chapter 26, God outlines the reward for obedience, and the punishment for disobedience. In four separate verses, God says He will punish His people for their sins, 'SEVEN TIMES OVER' (v. 18, 21, 24, 27). God confirms His Word that the people of Israel would suffer a terrible famine in the land before being defeated by the enemy and exiled – scattered among the nations. The cities would be ruined, Jerusalem and the temple destroyed, and the land lie desolate as evidence of God's wrath upon His disobedient and sinful nation.

> **"The whole land will be a burning waste of salt and sulfur – nothing planted, nothing sprouting, no vegetation growing on it. It will be like the destruction of Sodom and Gomorrah... All the nations will ask: "Why has the Lord done this to this land? Why this fierce, burning anger? And the answer will be: "It is because this people abandoned the covenant of the Lord, the God of their fathers, the covenant he made with them when he brought them out of Egypt."** (Deut. 30:23-25)

How long is seven 'times'? In the Bible, a 'time' usually refers to a year, for example in the book of Daniel, King Nebucchadnezzar loses his mind and lives as a wild beast, eating grass like cattle 'until seven times pass by him' (Dan. 4:25). This was understood to be seven years of time. In terms of days, this is 360 calendar

The Set Time for Mercy on Zion 115

days multiplied by 7 years = 2,520 days. Although a 'day' may be an appropriate punishment for an individual, a 'day' is sometimes exchanged for a 'year' for a nation. For example, the spies who returned with an evil report about the land, causing Israel to lose heart brought a punishment – a year for each day – for the forty days that the spies checked out the land, the nation would wander for forty years in the wilderness. The seven 'times' of punishment upon Israel, then, (2,520 days) could very well last 2,520 years. When did the punishment begin? Jerusalem was completely destroyed and the Jews taken captive to Babylon in the year 606 B.C.E. If the punishment were to last 2,520 years, this would take us to the year 1914. If we allow for several years leeway to accommodate the time it took to accomplish the exile of the Jews, we can still see that the punishment of Israel ended in this century. What world event happened in 1914? World War I began and launched the events leading to the Balfour Declaration, giving legitimacy to the re-birth of the nation of Israel. Also, at this time, Britain conquered the Turks, gaining control of the area of Palestine. I believe exact dates are not as important as understanding the general time period of the punishment and its end. All the signs indicate that *it has ended in our very generation.*

Times of the Gentiles Fulfilled

Yeshua also gave us clues as to the time of the end of the punishment upon Israel:

> **"For this is the time of punishment in fulfillment of all that has been written...They will fall by the sword and will be taken as prisoners to all the nations. Jerusalem will be trampled on by the Gentiles until the times of the Gentiles are fulfilled."**
> (Luke 21:24)

Yeshua indicated that Jerusalem would come under Gentile, foreign domination for a specific period of time – UNTIL – the times of the Gentiles are fulfilled.

When did this city, Jerusalem, return to Jewish control? This miracle happened in 1967, when Israeli soldiers, after an incredibly swift victory, reached 'the Wall' – the only remaining structure of the once magnificent Temple. Jerusalem, in our generation, is no longer under Gentile control.

Is it possible that the times of the Gentiles are fulfilled? Is this why the Holy Spirit is moving so powerfully in the Church to restore the awareness of the Jewish roots of Christianity at this time? Paul also tells us that

> **"Israel has experienced a hardening in part until the full number of the Gentiles has come in. And so all Israel will be saved, as it is written, 'The deliverer will come from Zion, he will turn godlessness away from Jacob and this is my covenant with them when I take away their sins."** (Rom. 11:25-27)

The scriptures indicate that we have reached the fullness or the end of the 'times of the Gentiles'. Does this mean that Gentiles are no longer being gathered into the Kingdom? Of course not, but the Lord is doing a new thing, and it involves Israel and the Jewish people. The Holy Spirit is making the blind to see and the deaf to hear. More Jewish people are recognizing their Messiah than ever before. We are entering a new era for Israel. God is preparing to turn godlessness away from Jacob and to take away her sins. The appointed time of her restoration has come.

The word of God contains another 'until' that gives us a sign as to the times we are living in: Yeshua is prophesied to remain in heaven UNTIL a set time at which He will return to earth and fulfill the remaining prophecies.

> **"He (Yeshua) must remain in heaven until the time comes for God to restore everything, as he promised long ago through his holy prophets."** (Acts 3:21)

When is this time? The time of restoration, spoken of by all the prophets. This can only be the restoration of Israel. Yeshua said that when the fig tree (representing Israel) begins to bud and show forth leaves, his return is near. (Matt. 24:32-33) He is not at the outskirts of the city, or somewhere in the vicinity, He is 'right at the door'.

The Budding of the Fig Tree

What do we currently see happening in the land of Israel indicating the budding of the fig tree? In 1948, the world witnessed its physical re-birth.

> **"Can a country be born in a day or a nation be brought forth in a moment? Yet no sooner is Zion in labor than she gives birth to her children."** (Is. 66:8)

Since this time, an ecological miracle has taken place; the desert wasteland is blossoming:

> **"The desert and the parched land will be glad; the wilderness will rejoice and blossom."** (Is. 34:1)

I hope that many of you will one day come to the land to witness the beautiful miracle God is accomplishing in restoring the land. As I walk my son to school, I am continually amazed and refreshed by the beauty of the gardens in this settlement. Lattice entrances to people's homes lie heavy laden with royal purple morning glories, forming a kind of chupah (wedding canopy), as if just waiting for the day of the arrival of the Bridegroom for His Bride. Rock gardens overflow with flowers of every color and variety; truly it is magnificent – like the Garden of Eden:

> **"The Lord will surely comfort Zion and will look with compassion on all her ruins; He will make her deserts like Eden, her wastelands like the garden of the Lord."** (Is. 51:3)

Why does seeing these gardens fill me with such hope and joy? It is not only because of their natural beauty, but because I know from the word of God that this is only the first stage of his restoration plan for Israel.

> **"My righteousness draws near speedily, my salvation (Yeshua) is on the way."** (Is. 51:5)

Yes, Yeshua is already on His way to save Israel. The restoration of the land is first, next comes the return of the exiles, then finally the spiritual restoration of the Israeli people's hearts to God.

> **"For the Israelites will live many days without king or prince, without sacrifices or sacred stones, without ephod or idol. Afterward the Israelites will return and seek the Lord their God and David their king. They will come trembling to the Lord and to his blessings in the last days."** (Hos. 3:4-5)

'David their king' refers to the Messiah from the line of King David who will rule over His throne forever. This, of course, describes the blessed and long awaited reconciliation between

God and His people. The book of Hosea describes God's intense love for Israel, as a devoted husband loves his adulterous wife. Despite her episodes of unfaithfulness, he refuses to give her up.

> **"How can I give you up, Ephraim? How can I hand you over, Israel? My heart is changed within me; all my compassion is aroused. I will not carry out my fierce anger, nor will I turn and devastate Ephraim. For I am God, and not man – the Holy One among you. I will not come in wrath. They will follow the Lord; he will roar like a lion (of Judah). When he roars, his children will come trembling from the west…I will settle them in their homes," declares the Lord."** (Hos. 11:8-11)

Like the prodigal father, he agonizes over his stubborn, wayward son, but waits and longs for his return. When Israel returns to the Lord, even while the son is still a long way off, the Father will see him and be filled with compassion for him; he will run towards him and kiss his offspring. A great celebration will be declared over the spiritual resurrection of Israel.

> **"Let's have a feast and celebrate. For this son of mine was dead and is alive again; he was lost and is found.' So they began to celebrate."** (Luke 15:24)

Gentile brothers and sisters of this beloved son, Ephraim, need not become angry over what may seem like preferential treatment.

> **"The older brother became angry and refused to go in."** (Luke 15: 28)

The father says that you are always with him and everything

he has is yours. But if you continue in a negative attitude towards the Jews, despite their current behavior, you will surely miss out on a wonderful party. And it will be your loss,

> **"Because his brother of yours was dead and is alive again; he was lost and is found."** (Luke 15:32)

It will soon be time to rejoice and be glad over the spiritual re-birth of the people of Israel, but unless Gentile Christians understand their relationship to their Jewish brothers and sisters through the Messiah, they will miss out on the joy and celebration that God has for them.

What other signs do we see indicating that we are now in the time of restoration?

The mountains of Israel are producing branches and fruit in preparation for the return of God's people Israel. Today, many Jewish settlements live and thrive on these mountains:

> **"But you, O mountains of Israel, will produce branches and fruit for my people Israel, for they will soon come home."** (Ezek. 36:8)

Israel is exporting fruit and flowers to the world:

> **"In days to come Jacob will take root, Israel will bud and blossom and fill all the world with fruit."** (Is. 27:6)

The exiles of Israel are returning to the land from all four corners of the earth:

> "Do not be afraid, for I am with you; I will bring your children from the east and gather you from the west, I will say to the north, 'Give them up!' and to the south, 'Do not hold them back.' Bring my sons from afar and my daughters from the ends of the earth." (Is. 43:5-6)

The towns and cities are being inhabited and re-built; children play in the streets.

> **"The towns will be inhabited and the ruins rebuilt."** (Ezek. 36:10)

> **"The streets of the city shall be full of boys and girls playing in its streets."** (Zech. 8:5)

We just finished celebrating Yom Kippur (Day of Atonement) in Israel. Although the majority of the Israeli population is secular, on this holiest day of the year, not even one car dares to drive on the streets of this settlement. For the children it is a great treat. They all play and rollerblade and bike up and down the streets. I tell my youngest son that every time he is out playing with his friends in the streets of Israel, he is fulfilling the prophetic word of God. That brings a beautiful smile!

Say to Zion...Your God is Here!

Yes, the restoration of the nation of Israel is well on its way: The time of the punishment is at an end; the seven 'times' are over. The Times of the Gentiles have been fulfilled; the set time to favor Zion has come. What word are we to speak to God's people, Israel? Many of them today are disillusioned, weary, cynical, frustrated, and sometimes fearful – what are we instructed to 'say to Zion'; at this point in time?

> "Say to the Daughter of Zion, 'See, your Savior comes!'" (Is. 62:11)

Do you want beautiful feet? Join us in driving up the mountains of Israel to bring to the cities of Judah the good news of salvation.

> "How beautiful on the mountains are the feet of those who bring good news, who proclaim peace, who bring good tidings, who proclaim salvation, who say to Zion, "Your God reigns!" (Is. 52:7)

We do not stand on street corners passing out Christian tracts about Jesus (although perhaps some are called to do that). Instead, we went up on a high mountain, as God commands, through the guarded, barbed wire gates of the Jewish towns, surrounded by hostile Arabic villages, and sang to Zion of salvation through their God, the King of Israel (Is. 40:9).

The word of God tells us to encourage and strengthen them with assurance that GOD – who is mighty and powerful – El Gibor v'haNorah – is on their side. Just like at the time of Purim, He is coming to save and deliver His people.

> "Strengthen the feeble hands, steady the knees that give way; say to those with fearful hearts, "Be strong, do not fear your God will come, he will come with vengeance with divine retribution he will come to save you." (Is. 35:3-4)

Now is the time to speak comfort to God's people, to assure them that the time of the punishment is over:

> "Comfort, comfort my people, says your God. Speak tenderly to Jerusalem, and proclaim to her that her hard service has been completed, that her sin has been paid for, that she has received from the Lord's hand double for all her sins." (Is. 40:1-2)

CHAPTER NINE

God - The Covenant Keeper

Even during the terrible time of punishment, however, God makes it clear that He **did not** break covenant with His people.

> "I will remember my covenant with Jacob and my covenant with Isaac and my covenant with Abraham, and I will remember the land…They will pay for their sins because they rejected my Torah and abhorred my decrees. Yet in spite of this, when they are in the land of their enemies, I will not reject them or abhor them so as to destroy them completely, breaking my covenant with them. I am the Lord their God. But for their sake, I will remember the covenant with their ancestors whom I brought out of Egypt in the sight of the nations to be their God. I am Yehovah." (Lev. 26:42-45)

God never has and never will reject or abandon His people Israel, no matter what they do or have done.

> "Only if the heavens above can be measured and the foundations of the earth below be searched out will I reject all the descendants of Israel because of all they have done." (Jer. 31:37)

It is vital, in this hour, that all Bible believing people understand this Truth.

The Scarlet Cord - Salvation for Rahab

Our only hope as we quickly approach the 'Day of the Lord' is to stand with God and with Israel when she will surely come under terrible attack. Remember that it was only Rahab and her family who were spared out of the entire city of Jericho when Joshua, under the leadership of the Lord destroyed everyone within the city walls. After hiding the Israelites spies, she requested of them,

> "Now then, please swear to me by the Lord that you will show kindness to my family, because I have shown kindness to you." (Josh. 2:12)

Rahab, a prostitute, could not trust in her own righteousness. She was spared simply because she feared the God of Israel, and knew that she needed to do whatever was in her power to demonstrate that she chose to ally herself with Israel, God's people. She gave shelter to the Israelite spies and was saved. When Rahab asked for a sure sign that she and her father and mother, brothers and sisters, and all who belong to them would be spared, the spies directed her to tie a scarlet cord in the window. Why a scarlet cord? This scarlet cord represents the blood covenant, by which we find salvation. It is the unifying cord, running the length of the Bible – salvation through the blood, Yeshua. When the wall of Jericho collapsed, every living thing in the city – men and women, young and old, cattle, sheep and donkeys, were all destroyed. But regarding Rahab, Joshua promised:

> **"Only Rahab the prostitute and all who are with her in her house shall be spared, because she hid the spies we sent."** (Josh. 6:17)

Rahab showed mercy to Israel; therefore God showed mercy to her and her loved ones.

Separating Sheep and Goats

Notice the warning of the Lord in Matthew 25:31-46. This section of scripture deals with the Son of Man sitting on his throne and judging the peoples. He separates the sheep, whom He calls righteous and directs into their reward – eternal life, from the goats, whom He calls cursed, sending them to eternal punishment. How does he separate the sheep from the goats? His judgment is based upon what the people did or did not do for his brothers. Who are His brothers? To whom did He say He was sent? To the lost sheep of the house of Israel (Matthew 15:24). Therefore, 'the least of these brothers of His are the Jews. Did the majority of the people of 'Christian' Europe give food, drink and shelter to dying Jews trapped in cattle cars during the Holocaust? Did they visit those imprisoned in concentration camps to give medical aid, clothing, or even a word of comfort? Certainly a few conscientious people hid some Jewish people or helped them to escape. These will be called righteous by the Lord, as they are called 'The Righteous Gentiles' at Yad Vashem, the Holocaust Museum in Jerusalem. But what of the rest? I believe that God will give His true people a redeeming opportunity to help the Jewish people escape the coming persecution. Be prepared to give food, shelter, clothing, medical aid and refuge.

> "The King will reply, 'I tell you the truth, whatever you did for one of the least of these brothers of mine, you did for me." (Matt. 25:40)

Chuck & Ted

Before moving to Israel, I heard a cassette tape recorded by Chuck, a Messianic Jewish Pastor of a congregation in Jerusalem. In it, he describes a situation in which he and his family attempted to visit their family in the United States, but when they arrived at the Israeli airport, they were turned away. Apparently, the children's passports were expired. Chuck describes being devastated by this, completely out of proportion to the minor inconvenience of the delay. When his neighbor, Ted, a devoted Christian and the director of Be'ad Chaim (Pro-Life Israel) Ministry, saw that Pastor Cohen and his family had returned, he was surprised and inquired as to the situation. Ted and his wife, Linda, took the family in for a Shabbat (Sabbath) meal, and the next day, Sunday, they took care of all the bureaucratic steps necessary to update the children's passports (a miracle in Israel!), and paid for a taxi to take them back to the airport. That same night they were on the airplane destined for Grandma's. Pastor Cohen relates how he inquired of the Lord about his overreaction to the delay and God showed him a vision. In it, he saw a reverse situation - many Jewish people were attempting to leave the United States to get to Israel, but they were being turned away at the airport, leaving them completely devastated. The Lord revealed that only through the kindness of devoted Christians would the Jewish people succeed in getting out. This was one of many other messages that finally convinced us to make our move to Israel now. Little did I know that I would actually meet Chuck Cohen and Ted Walker on my very first day in the land of Israel at a Bead Chaim conference near Jerusalem. God is so good! He is always in control behind the scenes even if we cannot see Him in the midst of the chaos and darkness surrounding us.

Precious Christian, be prepared for how God will use you if you are willing. Yes, we are saved by grace through the blood of Yeshua, but, a dead faith cannot save.

> **"What good is it, my brothers, if a man claims to have faith but has no deeds? Can such faith save him?...Faith by itself, if it is not accompanied by action, is dead."** (James 2:14-17)

God makes it clear what He expects of us:

> **"To act justly and to love mercy and to walk humbly with your God."** (Mic. 6:8)

CHAPTER TEN

PERSONAL SALVATION THE NEW COVENANT

Yes, it may be too late to turn back the hand of God's judgment against our nations. But it is not too late for anyone to find mercy and personal salvation in the Lord through a wonderful new covenant of forgiveness, peace, healing, and restoration. This is the New Covenant, first promised to the house of Israel and the house of Judah.

> "The time is coming," declares the Lord, when I will make a new covenant with the house of Israel and with the house of Judah. It will not be like the covenant I made with their forefathers when I took them by the hand to lead them out of Egypt, because they broke my covenant, though I was a husband to them. This is the covenant I will make with the house of Israel after that time," declares the Lord. "I will put my law in their minds and write it on their hearts. I will be their God, and they will be my people... For I will forgive their wickedness and will remember their sins no more." (Jer. 31:31-34)

This beautiful covenant of forgiveness, grace, blessing, healing, prosperity and spiritual restoration of a relationship with God was sealed with the blood sacrifice of Yeshua. He said, while holding up the third cup of wine at their Passover Seder,

> **"This is my blood of the covenant, which is poured out for many."** (Mark 14:24)

Remember that only the blood makes atonement for our lives.

> **"It is the blood that makes atonement for one's life."** (Lev. 17:11)

and that all covenants are sealed with blood.

> **"In fact, the Torah required that nearly everything be cleansed with blood, and without the shedding of blood there is no forgiveness."** (Heb. 9:22)

What covenant was Yeshua referring to that would be sealed with his own blood? Certainly not the Mosaic Covenant of blessing or cursing – Moses had already sprinkled this with blood. The sacrifice had also been made for the Abrahamic Covenant. No, Yeshua was referring to this New Covenant – an everlasting promise of peace extended from a merciful God to a sinful people and undeserving people.

> **"So now I have sworn not to be angry with you, never to rebuke you again. Though the mountains be shaken and the hills be removed, yet my unfailing love for you will not be shaken nor my covenant of peace be removed," says the Lord, who has compassion on you."** (Is. 54:9-10)

Salvation is extended, not just to the Jews, but to any person of any race, tongue, tribe, age, or gender. When Peter received a vision from God, he understood its meaning and said,

> **"I now realize how true it is that God does not show favoritism but accepts men from every nation who fear him and do what is right."** (Acts 10:34)

Whether you are a Jew or Gentile, I urge you to pray from your heart:

> God of Israel, of Abraham, Isaac, and Jacob, I come to you and ask for your forgiveness for all of my sins. Please forgive me for _____ (include the specific sins that come to your mind such as cursing the Jewish people, practicing forms of paganism, disrespecting His Torah, or living a sinful lifestyle). Thank you for sending your own arm, the Messiah, Yeshua, to take the punishment that I deserve. I believe that He is the promised Messiah who died to atone for my sins. Please set me free from any curse I have brought upon myself or my family, and from every bondage to the kingdom of darkness. I want to live a life pleasing to you. Please give me a new heart and a new Spirit to obey you. Lead and guide me to do your will in these last days. Thank you for your salvation that you have provided through Yeshua, your son. Amen.

Note: If you prayed this prayer, and would like to contact the author, receive additional information, please visit our website: www.voiceforisrael.com or write to publisher for a current listing of available teaching materials.

CHAPTER ELEVEN

Mordechai's Call To Esther

We have covered in great depth God's plan of salvation for Israel and the Jewish people but where exactly does the Church fit in this plan? I believe that a divine Esther Call is going forth to the true Christian Church to wake up and to understand the urgency of the present time. Just as Vashti, a picture of the apostate church, lived in the house of the King, but was too occupied with her own 'party' to obey the summons, of the King, some churches are simply too busy with their own programs, and too stuck in their traditions to understand God's great plan in these last days! Vashti is compared in Scripture to Jezebel and is a rebellious spirit.

We are living in a momentous minute of history! We must keep our eyes fixed on the prophetic Word of God and our minds focused on His will. Believers worldwide are being given the privilege of participating in the resurrection from the dead of the people of Israel. We all need to seek the face of God for our part.

Esther is a picture of the true church which is faithful and obedient. Modechai symbolizes the Holy Spirit, who commands the Esther Church, to petition the King for the lives of Her people.

> "He told him to urge her to go into the king's presence to beg for mercy and plead with him for her people." (Esth. 4:8)

As Christians, covered in the blood of the Lamb, the privilege is offered to come boldly to the King's throne of Grace. His golden scepter is extended to His 'Beloved' – His special choice of Bride. When Esther hesitated, Mordechai rebuked her:

> "Do not think that because you are in the king's house you alone of all the Jews will escape." (Esth. 4:14)

I have heard far too many Christians express their belief that simply because they are 'in the king's household' they will escape the coming persecution through a magical 'pre-tribulation rapture'. The Jews, they consider, will then be left here on earth to suffer while they watch safely from the clouds. This is a grave deception and completely unfounded in scripture. The Lord makes it clear, as do other New Testament scriptures that He is not returning until AFTER the tribulation. (Matt. 24:29-30) It is at this time that He gathers His elect. Mordechai goes on to say to Esther,

> "For if you remain silent at this time, relief and deliverance for the Jews will arise from another place, but you and your father's family will perish." (Esth. 4:14)

Yes, the scriptures prove that God will save the Jews. Purim gives us an example of His mighty deliverance. But this is not time for 'Esther' to remain silent. All true Christians have been raised to a royal position:

> "But you are a chosen people, a royal priesthood, a holy nation, a people belonging to God, that you may declare the praises of him who called you out of darkness into his wonderful light. Once you were not a people, but now you are the people of God; once you had not received mercy, but now you have received mercy." (1 Pet 2:9)

Those who once did not know God's mercy, but have experienced his mercy; those who once were not God's people, but now belong to the family of God have a divine mission – a destiny for this final hour.

> **And who knows but that you have come to royal position for such a time as this?"** (Esth. 4:14)

What was Esther's response to Mordechai's request? She called for a time of fasting and prayer. Some churches and individuals are heeding the call of the Holy Spirit, and declaring an 'Esther Fast' at the time of Purim for the salvation of Israel and the Jews. If the Royal Priesthood will not stand in the gap for Israel, who will? Certainly not the world. Due to the threat of an Arab boycott, Disney World agreed to modify its Israeli exhibit in order that Jerusalem would not be presented as the capital of Israel. *'Shame on Mickey; shame on Disney"*, Abraham Foxman, director of the Anti-Defamation League said in a statement to the Jerusalem Post.[1]

Indeed, recent terror attacks by Islamic extremists have begun to alert the world to the serious threat of the Islamic Movement. The 9/11 attack on the twin towers in America acted as a wake up call. We cannot bow to economic or political pressure from Arabic, anti-Israel, anti-God coalitions. We can bow to only one

---

[1] *'Jerusalem Post'*, September 1999, pg. 1-2

God – the God of Israel, the God of Abraham, Isaac, and Jacob. Mordechai knew this. It was his refusal to bow to Haman that infuriated the anti-Semite and brought the threat of death to all Jews. But, just as God delivered the Jews of Persia; just as he shut the lion's mouths so that they would not harm Daniel in the lion's den; and just as He saved Daniel's three friends and even walked with them in the fiery furnace, we must trust God and never give in to the ungodly pressure to forsake God and His people.

The same spirit of Amalek that tried to destroy the Jewish people through Haman will rise again in the final hour. All nations will come against Israel and Jerusalem.

> **"I will gather all the nations to Jerusalem to fight against it."** (Zech. 14:2)

At Purim time, the edict of the King went out giving the Jews the right to defend themselves:

> **"To destroy, kill, and annihilate any armed force of any nationality or province that might attack them and their women and children; and to plunder the property of their enemies."** (Esth. 8:11)

This edict remains in effect. As I write this, I can hear the Muslims in the surrounding villages shouting through loudspeakers, calling for 'Jihad'. But if God be for us, who can stand against us? At Purim, the Jews were unbeatable.

> **"No one could stand against them."** (Esth. 9:2)

But just as at Purim, with the Lord on Israel's side, no one will be able to stand against her. God will make even the most feeble of men like the mighty King David.

> "On that day the Lord will shield those who live in Jerusalem, so that the feeblest among them will be like David, and the house of David will be like God, like the Angel of the lord going before them. On that day I will set out to destroy all the nations that attack Jerusalem." (Zech. 21:8-9)

The media and world opinion will continue to turn against Israel and the Jews. As individuals who know God, we must stand strong and be of courage. The dividing line is being drawn. No one will be allowed to sit on the fence. May our prayer be that God will give us the courage of Esther to stand with Israel and the Jewish people in the coming days. May we proclaim, as did Esther,

> "And if I perish, I perish." (Esth. 4:16)

God was so mighty through the Jews at Purim that many people actually converted to become Jews.

> "And many people of other nationalities became Jews because fear of the Jews had seized them." (Esth. 8:17)

In the last days, a similar phenomenon will take place:

> "In those days ten men from all languages And nations will take firm hold of one Jew by the hem of his robe and say, 'Let us go with you, because we have heard that God is with you." (Zech. 8:23)

Sorrow Turned to Joy

Purim can remind us that, just as what happened with the Jews of Persia who complete destruction, our sorrow will one day be turned to joy and our mourning into days of celebration.

> "Have them celebrate annually the fourteenth and fifteenth days of the month of Adar as the time when the Jews got relief from their enemies, and as the month when their sorrow was turned into joy and their mourning into a day of celebration...observe the days as days of feasting and joy and giving presents of food to one another and gifts to the poor." (Esth. 9:21-22)

One day, God will dwell in our midst as Immanu-El (God With Us), and He will wipe every tear from our eyes.

> "Then I saw a new heaven and a new earth, for the first heaven and the first earth had passed away, and there was no longer any sea. I saw the Holy City, the New Jerusalem, coming down out of heaven from God, prepared as a bride beautifully dressed for her husband. And I heard a loud voice from the throne saying, "Now the dwelling of God is with men, and he will live with them. They will be His people, and God himself will be with them and be their God. He will wipe every tear from their eyes. There will be no more death or mourning or crying or pain, for the old order of things has passed away." (Rev. 21:1-4)

God bless you and may you enjoy a very

Happy Purim!

APPENDIX I

Purim Customs, Traditions and Recipes

Traditionally, on Purim, Jewish people bake triangular shaped cookies called <u>Hamantaschen,</u> also called Oznei Haman in Hebrew, meaning the ears of Haman. These are sent, along with other treats, in little gift baskets to family and friends as well as to the poor and needy as commanded. **"...that they should make them days of feasting and joy, of sending presents to one another and gifts to the poor."** (Esther 9:22) This is called <u>Shalach Manot.</u> Remembering the poor is extremely important in God's sight and is specifically mentioned in several scriptures: **"He who has mercy on the poor, happy** (in Hebrew Ashrei – blessed, rich) **is he....He who oppresses the poor reproaches his Maker, but he who honors Him has mercy on the needy."** (Proverbs 14:21,31). It honors God to have mercy on the poor and needy; He richly repays those who heed this command. Perhaps a family could bake some hamentaschen and take a batch to elderly Jewish people in a local nursing home?

Shopping for prunes in Israel

I went to buy prunes to make hamentashen, the traditional triangular cookies for Purim (called oznei haman in Hebrew, meaning ears of Haman), but it was a struggle. First, I didn't know how to say prune in Hebrew. I was trying to tell them that I wanted the stuff to make my own hamentashen, but they kept showing me all the yucky ones they had already made, which are hard as rocks and not at all like mama used to make in Canada. Finally, we get to the prunes, and I learn the Hebrew word. (should have looked it up in the dictionary before I went). They told me prunes cost 33 sheckels a kilo and so i get 1/2 a kilo of these dried up looking prunes sealed in a plastic bag. I go into another store, and notice that he has beautiful, plump, prunes in bulk. So I ask how much and he says, 26 sheckels a kilo. Already I know I've been ripped off. I check how much are the little 'shalach munos' candy boxes for the kids. I shouldn't have asked. They're only 7.50 and guess how much I paid? Right - 11 sheckels. So I go back to the first store and ask if I can return the prunes at least. They never give you your money back here, but they did mark my name down for a credit towards my next purchase. Oh well. At least I got my prunes. I also got poppyseeds (pereg - I knew that one) and walnuts (egozim).

Shopping for groceries at the co-op yesterday was a real treat as well. I went in for just a few items, but as usual, filled the grocery cart various items we needed. We got off to a shaky start. I needed five sheckels for the cart and only had a 50 sheckel bill, so I asked for change at customer service. She wouldn't give me change, but asked me to leave my teudat zehut (identity card). I thought, 'Now this is getting ridiculous! I know you need a teudat zehut to do just about anything in Israel, but - for a grocery cart - you've got to be kidding me!' My husband, David, just about hit the roof! After everything we went through to get that card, he was not about to let it out of our possession, especially not to get a grocery cart. We have a little portable cart on wheels that will hold a few bags, so we took that in, but security stopped us, saying, "Asoor, asoor!" (not allowed!") I thought David was really going to lose it right there and then. Thankfully, the customer service (if you can call it that) clerk has mercy on us and decides to buck the system and give me change after all to get a grocery cart so I can collect my groceries.

O.K. You think that's the end of it. Right? wrong! We get to the checkout, and of course it was more than we expected to spend, so I didn't have enough cash on me. Neither was there enough to cover the full amount of 535 sheckels in the account. So I gave the cashier 200 sheckels in cash and wrote a cheque for

400, expecting her to give me the change in sheckels. Oh no, this would be too easy for Israel. The cashier had already punched in 200 cash, so the cheque was too much and she could not (for some vague reason) adjust her register, so they called over the manager, and they're hollering back and forth what to do about this dilemma. Meanwhile, the lineup behind us is getting longer and longer and the people more and more disgruntled. Finally, the manager decides what to do. (No, I didn't have another cheque, and no, I could not change the amount on the cheque and initial the changes. they don't accept that in Israel). The manager voids the whole transaction and starts all over again - ringing in every single item by the number codes. Everyone had to move to the next cashier. Groans....O.K., they accept it. Mah La-asot? (What can you do?) "No!No!", the cashier screams, after they've moved to the next cashier. "Cashier number seven!". So they all move again. (probably thinking, 'just another day in Israel') Can you imagine how long it took for her to ring in 535 sheckels worth of groceries again by number code?!

I was so exhausted when I got home. I think I might turn into one of those neurotic people that never leave their apartments. I'll never complain about customer service in Canada again.

Love Hannah

Hamentashen Cookie Dough

3 eggs	½ c. water
1 c. oil	½ c. orange juice
1 c. sugar	1/8 tsp. salt
2 tsp baking powder	4 c. flour (approximately)

Combine ingredients in order given, using enough flour to make a soft dough which is not sticky. Let stand 15 minutes. Divide into 4 parts. Roll to ¼" thickness on a floured board. Cut into 4" circles. Place a spoonful of desired filling in the centre of each circle. Form triangles by folding sides in towards the middle. Brush with beaten egg. Bake on a lightly greased baking sheet at 350 for 30 minutes, until golden brown. Yield: about 5 dozen.

Prune filling

1 lb. prunes, stewed, pitted& chopped
½ lemon, juice and rind
1 c. raisings, shopped
¼ c. bread crumbs
¼ c. chopped nuts
½ c. sugar
1 tbsp. honey

Combine all ingredients and mix thoroughly.

Poppy seed filling

½ lb. poppy seed	2 tbsp. sugar
4 tbsp. honey	juice of ½ lemon

Soak the poppy seed in boiling water overnight. Drain, dry and grind through food chopper, using finest blade. Add remaining ingredients and mix well.

Note: Any kind of jam or alternate filling may also be used. Our children love to use nutella, a chocolate and nut based spread in their hamentashen. Be sure to let the children help make these!

On the eve of Purim, the book of Esther is read as a congregation, with the children dressing up in costumes and drowning out the name of Haman whenever it is mentioned with loud boo's and swinging their groggers (noisemakers), called a ra'ashan in Hebrew from the word ra'ash which means noise. A drama is often performed re-enacting the story of Esther. Afterwards, a time of feasting, rejoicing and celebration is held by the community. " ... **as the month which was turned from sorrow to joy for them, and from mourning to a holiday; that they should make them days of feasting and joy...**" (Esther 9:22)

Purim crafts

Home made grogger (noisemaker)

Put a handful of popping corn into a large, empty juice can (with only 2 holes at the top that were used for pouring). Trace the base of the can onto a cardboard. Cut the cardboard and trim the circle so it fits snugly onto the side of the can. Decorate the can by covering it with felt and gluing it on with household cement to also cover the holds so corn can't escape. Add decorations and coloring with felts. Use groggers to drown out the name of the villain, Haman, and by stamping, yelling, and general ra'ash (noise). A stop and go sign can be used by the leader to help control the bedlam and continue the reading of the megilla (book of Esther).

Purim Masks: Using balloons and paper mache, masks of the queen, king, and Haman can be created and worn as part of a costume.

Purim Intercession:

This is also a wonderful opportunity to gather as a Body of Messiah with other like-minded people of one heart, to intercede to the King of Kings and Lord of Lords for the lives and souls of the Jewish people, especially those left in the nations of the earth. Let us plead, as did Esther, **"How can I endure to see the evil that will come to my people? Or how can I endure to see the destruction of my country men?"** (Esther 8:6) Let us also take time to fast and pray, coming boldly to the King's throne of grace to plead mercy and help in this critical hour! As His Bride, we have been given full authority to use His signet ring and to seal any decree in His name. This decree cannot be revoked. It is His Church that has been given authority to do so and we must rise up to put this God-given authority into use.

"You yourselves write a decree concerning the Jews, as you please, in the king's name, and seal it with the king's signet ring; for whatever is written in the king's name and sealed with the king's signet ring no one can revoke." (Esther 8:8) Did not Yeshua tell us that **whatever we ask the Father in His name, He shall give to us!** (John 16:23)

For it is not our bow nor shall our own sword save us, but through our God we shall do valiantly. It is He who shall tread down our enemies!

> **For I will not trust in my bow, nor shall my sword save me, but You have saved us from our enemies, and have put to shame those who hated us. In God we boast all day long, and praise Your name forever."** (Psalm 44:6-8)

APPENDIX II

The following is a copy of an e-mail correspondance.

March 8th, 2001
Shalom from Jerusalem:

Satan Wears A Kippah?

We just returned from celebrating Purim at the neighborhood synagogue in Israel. We attended the conservative synagogue because it is basically an American movement, with many native English speakers. Conservative Jews are fighting for equal rights in Israel with the Orthodox. A large sign at the front of the auditorium read, "There is more than one way to be a Jew." The irony is that even within the Conservative or Reform movements, who are themselves persecuted by the Orthodox their multi-pathway to 'being a Jew' does generally not include those of 'The Way' (followers of Yeshua). During the service people took turns chanting in Hebrew the megillah (scroll) of Esther. The scene in the synagogue would actually have been hilarious - if it wasn't so sad. A witch in a black miniskirt greeted us at the door. We noticed her throughout the service, bowing her head and 'dovening' (praying) diligently. Next to her was a druid, goblin looking character with an evil mask. Among the crowd were several 'demons'. The one in particular which caught my eye represented 'satan', but with a kippah (men's headcovering) clipped to the hair of the mask. What a contradiction in terms: the kippah, meant to represent one's submission and devotion of the God of Israel, clipped to a representation of the king of the kingdom of darkness! Amidst all of this were several pretty little Queen Esthers in their miniature gowns and sparkling tiaras.

This shows just how far the people of Israel are from understanding our God. Even as they cheered Mordechai and 'booed' Haman, feasted and made merry as commanded on Purim, some masqueraded as agents of darkness, in complete ignorance that this could possibly be offensive to God. It's amazing to see how warped and twisted things have become. What most Jewish people believe is offensive to God is anything 'Christian'. I'll never forget when I taught private English lessons in Ariel and one of my students came to class with an 'alien' necklace around his neck. I tried, in very simple language, to explain to this native Israeli boy about the kingdom of darkness and the kingdom of light. He raised his fist in a victory sign and declared that God is the winner. Yes, I agreed,

"But this necklace you're wearing represents something that is very much against God", I continued.

He looked quite worried and said,

"You mean... Yeshu...?", making the symbol of the cross with his two fingers. (Yeshu is not a short form of Yeshua, which means salvation, but is a derogatory derivative which stands for 'may his name be blotted out for ever and ever.' Many Jewish people, when sharing with them about the Messiah, Yeshua, will say, "Do you mean Yeshu?" We must make it clear that His name is Yeshua and He is the One who saves us from our sins)

APPENDIX III

The following is a copy of a letter sent to several business owners in the settlement of Ariel, Israel.

Protesting Hallowe'en In Ariel

March 8th, 2000
To the residents and business owners of Ariel:

This letter concerns a serious problem, not only within Ariel, but nation-wide. That is, the blatant replacement of the Biblically Jewish holiday of Purim, with the pagan, festival of Hallowe'en. As a new immigrant to Israel from Canada, I must confess that I am appalled, aggravated, and angry at the way most stores are filled with Hallowe'en masks and costumes. We thought that we were bringing our children to Israel to be raised as Jews, but instead find Israel adopting the customs of the nations. If we wanted to live and celebrate as the nations do, we could have stayed in Canada and saved ourselves a whole lot of trouble and expense.

The Torah makes it clear that we, the nation of Israel, are not to take on the ways and customs of the nations around us.

> **"You must not worship Adonai your G-d in their way."** (Deut. 12:4)

יהוה (YHVH) has chosen us and set us apart, to be a holy nation unto Him.

> **"For you are a people holy to Adonai your God. Adonai your God has chosen you out of all the peoples on the face of the earth to be his people, his treasured possession."** (Deut. 7:6)

We are not to imitate the pagans. This is, and always has been an abomination to God, and was one of the reasons for our exile from our homeland. Will we never learn our lessons? Did we not pay a high enough price for our sins? We were persecuted, exiled, and murdered in all the lands to which Hashem scattered us. Why do we continue to repeat our mistakes like a dog returns to its vomit?

Purim celebrates G-d's miraculous deliverance of His people from the anti-Semite, Haman, in ancient Persia. Halloween, however, originates in the Druid new year celebration called Soween, or Samhain, which worships the god of the dead and his kingdom. The Druids were the influential priests, magicians and sorcerers of the Nature religions that prevailed in early Northern Europe. יהוה *hates the magic and sorcery of the heathens and forbids His people from participating in these practices or religions, especially in the land of Israel.*

> **"When you come into the land which the Lord your G-d is giving you, you shall not learn to follow the abominations of those nations."** (Deut 18:9)

Ancient Druids worshipped the Baal god as their king. Many Israelites of the time made the same tragic mistake. In the Torah, the prophet Eliyahu challenged these false prophets of Baal to a kind of spiritual duel. Whoever's G-d could call down fire from heaven to consume the sacrifice would prove to be the one, true, Almighty Elohim. We know the ending of the story. It was the God of Israel who consumed the sacrifice by fire, even though it was drenched with water, while the false god, Baal, was mute, asleep, or 'away on vacation', as Eliyahu taunted. The people fell on their faces, crying out, **"Adonai, hu HaElohim, Adonai, hu HaElohim (The Lord He is God)"** (1 Kings 18:39) *finally acknowledging G-d for who He really is. Eliyahu and the people* *who had turned back to Hashem seized the prophets of Baal and slaughtered them.*

Eliyahu challenged the people with a bold question that I believe applies to us today, "How long will you waver between two opinions? If Adonai is God, follow Him, but if Baal, follow him." How long will we waver between being the Jewish nation we were called to be - a light unto the nations - and being a cheap imitation of the other nations? How long will stores all over Israel be filled with masks and costumes representing Hasatan? Is it because we don't take him seriously? Job did. Is it because we don't take the Torah seriously? We should. The re-birth of the modern state of Israel is proof that Torah speaks the Truth and is the divine Word of God. Why, then, do we allow our stores to sell costumes to our children for them to dress up as every evil, ghoulish figure imaginable, rather than in costumes that would honor יהוה *(YHVH)? Why is the Rabbinate of Ariel not doing anything to correct this deplorable situation?*

How dare we, a holy nation, a chosen people, turn Purim into Halloween!

God will not tolerate this situation forever:

> **"What you have in your mind shall never be, when you say, we will be like the Goyim (Gentiles), like the families in other countries, serving wood and stone (and celebrating Hallowe'en...)"**

Realistically, I don't expect anyone to listen to this lone voice crying out in the wilderness. But whether anyone listens or fails to listen is not my responsibility. I write this letter simply to serve as warning that God will judge us for our actions. One day, Lord will cleanse this land from every abomination, every idol, and every wicked and evil thing, along with the rebellious who participate. But He is not unjust. He does not take pleasure in the death of anyone, but His desire is that all would repent, turn back to Him, and live.

I would like to see even one storekeeper, one shop owner, one manager with enough courage and fear of God to send every evil mask and costume back to where they came from - or better yet - burn them. Why don't we rise up as a community, the city of Ariel, and take a stand for God by banishing Hallowe'en from our midst and returning to a pure and joyful celebration of Purim.

"The fear of Adonai is the beginning of wisdom."
(Prov. 9:10)

APPENDIX IV

Pictures and Shadows of Purim (Feast of Lots)
Lessons for all Believers devoted to the one true God, hvhy,
And His Son, Yeshua

Esther – A picture of the true Church: obedient, (2:20) faithful, willing to lose her life, respectful of authority, courageous, beautiful, walking in humility, fasting and praying, seeking God. In covenant with the Jewish people but this relationship is not generally known by most others. Carries the full authority of the King and His signet ring to issue decrees that cannot be revoked. (Esther 8:8) Anointed with oil of myrrh (symbolic of suffering) as well as beautifying preparations and perfumes (Esther 2:12) The suffering we go through purifies and beautifies us.

Vashti – A picture of the false Church: lives in the King's house (Palace) but occupied with her own agenda (party); too concerned with her own self-seeking activities to obey the summons from the King. (1:12) Beauty is only superficial – looks good on the outside but rotten inside. Rebellious towards authority (Husband, pastor, Holy Spirit) A type of Jezebel. (Rev. 2:20). Encourages contempt for authority in others – her rebellion is contagious. Will be banished from the Kingdom in shame due to her rebellion and disobedience, pride. Her royal position will be given to another who is better than she." (Esther 1:19)

Mordechai – A picture of the Holy Spirit – He adopts and raises the church in God's ways (Esther 2:7); instructs, teaches, leads and guides into all truth; instructs when to speak and when to remain silent; (2:10; 4:14) faithfully watches over the Bride of the King – stands outside the gate; hovers over us to keep tabs on us (2:11) protective; privy to all secret information (the plot against the king). Intercedes for God's people with groanings. (Esther

4:1) (Romans 8:26) Gives direction to the church and convicts of sin (Do not remain silent....). Will not bow down to the enemy. Will not be moved. Partners with Esther (the church) to carry out the authority of the King.

Haman – A picture of the anti-Christ – the same spirit of Amalek that as in Pharaoh and in Hitler and today operates in Islam that wants full subjugation of all God's people to the powers of darkness. The pride of his heart has deceived him (Obadaiah 1:3)

Lessons from the book of Esther:
1. God is always at work behind the scenes (God's name not mentioned in book of Esther)
2. It's not over till it's over – Haman thought his evil plan was as good as done!
3. We have been called to royal position for such a time as this (1 Pet 2:9) – the moral responsibility of the Church to intercede for the lives and souls of people
4. Whatever evil people do to us will return upon their own heads – trust God to bring justice in His way and His timing & to intervene to prevent evil schemes from coming to pass against His people.
5. Obedience will cost us and will cost others – because Mordechai refused to bow to Haman, all the Jewish people were in danger of destruction.

Prayer Points:

Thanksgiving:

- That God has made us to be a Royal Kingdom of priests (cohanim) 1 Peter 2:9 to intercede for people
- That we have been born for such a time as this (Esther 4:14)

- That we have a voice and can speak up for those being led to the slaughter (If you remain silent…. (watchmen on the walls do not keep silent until…Isa. 62:6)
- That we can trust God is working behind the scenes to bring salvation & deliverance
- That we are all members of the commonwealth of Israel and equal heirs, One new man in Messiah; partakers of the covenants of promise, (Eph. 2:11-18)
- That the King has given us full authority to write out our own decree <u>in His name</u> and seal it with His signet ring (Esther 8:8)
- That the battle is the Lord's – deliverance and salvation is from Him (Psalm 44:4-7)

<u>Petitioning the King</u>:

- Boldly: **"Let us therefore come boldly to the throne of grace, that we may obtain mercy and find grace to help in time of need**." (Hebrews 4:16)
- With confidence that our prayers will be answered (John 16:23)
- Desperately and passionately: **"For how can I bear to see the evil/destruction that will come upon my people?"** (Esther 8:6)

<u>Requests:</u> As Esther pleaded with the King for mercy for the Jewish people.

- That Yehovah Tz'vaot (God of heavenly armies) will come to the aid and defense of the Jewish people who have been left in the nations and those presently in Israel from all anti-Semites and forces of destruction.
- That every evil plan and scheme of the enemy against God's people will be frustrated, brought to nothing,

annulled, made of no effect, returned upon their own heads.
- That the Jewish people will turn back to God with a spirit of grace and supplication, with weeping and lamentation and put their trust in Him and recognize His Son, Yeshua as the Jewish Messiah. "**And I will pour on the house of David and on the inhabitants of Jerusalem the Spirit of grace and supplication; then they will look on Me whom they pierced. Yes, they will mourn for Him as one mourns for his only son, and grieve for Him as one grieves for a firstborn.**" (Zech. 12:10)
- That they will not only be saved physically but also spiritually for eternity.
- That the Israeli Defense Force (IDF) and Jews of every city in the Diaspora (outside Israel) will gather together to protect themselves from anti-Semitism; to rise up in the spirit of David to "**destroy, kill, and completely wipe out the armies of any nation or state who attacks them.** (Esther 8:11) "**In that day I will seek to destroy all the nations that come against Jerusalem.**" (Zech. 12:9)
- That the feeblest among them will be like the mighty King David
- "**In that day the Lord will defend the inhabitants of Jerusalem; the one who is feeble among them in that day shall be like David…**
- That God, in His mercy, will raise up the true Esther Church and open her eyes to the revelation of His heart for Israel and the Jewish people. She will stand with Israel like Ruth with Naomi, an 'unto death' commitment borne out of love.
- That the fear of the Lord will come upon the enemies of Israel (even potential Islamic suicide bombers) so that

they will join our side. (Esther 8:17)
- "Thus says the Lord of Hosts: In those days ten men from every language of the nations shall grasp the sleeve of a Jewish man, saying, "Let us go with you, for we have heard that God is with you." (Zech 8:23)
- That even the spoil of the enemy will come into the hands of God's people(Esther 8:11)
- That the angel Michael, one of the chief princes, will come to help defeat the Prince of Persia. (Daniel 10:13)
- That God in heaven would reveal any secret plots of the wicked to His people (Daniel 2:19,28)
- That God's people would have the courage not to bow to anything or anyone other than God. (Daniel 3:12)

May these decrees be written in the name above all names, Yeshua Hamashiach (Jesus the Messiah) and sealed with the signet ring of the King of Kings and Lord of Lords.

To contact the Author write:

Hannah Nesher, Voice for Israel
Suite #313- 11215 Jasper Ave.
Edmonton, Alberta
T5K 0L5 Canada

www.voiceforisrael.net

*Please include your testimony or help received
from this book when you write.*

Your prayer requests are welcome

Additional Teaching Materials by Hannah Nesher

DVDs

Shalom Morah I (Hebrew for Christians & Hebrew Names of God) 11 DVD set

Shalom Morah II (Hebrew for Christians & Wisdom in the Hebrew Alphabet) 10 DVD set

Exploring the Jewish Roots of the Christian Faith

Unity in the Messiah

Because He Lives

Messianic Jewish Wedding in Jerusalem

There is a God in Israel

Messianic Jewish Passover

Passover Lamb or Easter Ham?

Voice Out of Zion II (Where is Your Brother Jacob?)

Walking Through the Wilderness

Ruth: A Righteous Gentile

Messiah in Chanukah

BOOKS

Grafted in Again

Journey to Jerusalem

Come Out of Her My People

Messiah Revealed in the Sabbath

Messiah Revealed in Passover

Messiah Revealed in the Fall Feasts

Messiah Revealed in Chanukah

Kashrut: The Biblical Dietary Laws

Messiah Revealed in Shavuot

You Know My Heart (English booklet)

You Know My Heart (Hebrew booklet)

If you enjoyed this book and would like to learn more, don't miss the companion DVD

VOICE OUT OF ZION II
Where is Your Brother Jacob?

It is time that the dark past of Christian history in relation to the Jewish people is brought into the Light. The tragic fact is that much of the persecution, torture, and martyrdom of the Jewish people has been at the hands of those who called themselves Christians. This breach has caused the dividing wall of hostility and fear that Jesus died to tear down between Jew and Gentile (Eph. 2:14) to be rebuilt. It has caused the Jews to turn away from their own Messiah and to see the cross as a symbol of hatred, brutality and butchery rather than the sign of God's redeeming love for His people. It is time to hear the truth that will bring forth a Godly sorrow and repentance that will help to heal the breach and restore the devastation of many generations.

Hannah teaches on location at Yad Vashem, the Holocaust Memorial Musuem, in Jerusalem, on Yom Zikaron Hashoah, Holocaust Memorial Day. See heart stirring images from the concentration camps in Poland and join with the people of Israel who grieve over their losses and yet honor the righteous Gentiles who helped them in their time of trouble.

Hannah Nesher, Voice for Israel
Suite #313- 11215 Jasper Ave.
Edmonton, Alberta
T5K 0L5 Canada
www.voiceforisrael.net

www.ingramcontent.com/pod-product-compliance
Lightning Source LLC
LaVergne TN
LVHW051604070426
835507LV00021B/2754